"Compelling. A must-read for any helping professional or loved one of a person momentarily swept up in the 'perfect storm' of childhood sexual abuse, intimacy problems, and eating disorders. Thornton's memoir reminds that there is hope and meaning after the storm."

—LINDA T. SANFORD, LICSW
AUTHOR OF *STRONG AT THE BROKEN PLACES* AND
ASSISTANT PROFESSOR, SIMMONS COLLEGE OF SOCIAL WORK

"A story of triumph and spiritual awakening that is bound to captivate readers. Candid, insightful, and inspirational."

—VIOLA FODOR, BED, MED
PSYCHOTHERAPIST, EDUCATOR, AND
AUTHOR OF *DESPERATELY SEEKING SELF*

"A gripping account of the absolute darkness and imprisonment brought on by self-destructive behaviour. Thornton effectively illustrates the vicious cycle of an eating disorder as she spirals into the 'hellhole' of depression, providing valuable insights into the struggle and inner turmoil stemming from childhood sexual abuse. I commend Thornton on having the courage to share her story to help others. She is living proof that there is triumph after adversity."

—MELINDA HUTCHINGS
AUTHOR OF *FIGHTING FOR LIFE: ANOREXIA—THE ROAD TO RECOVERY*
AND *HOW TO RECOVER FROM ANOREXIA AND OTHER EATING DISORDERS*
FOUNDER OF WWW.BODYCAGE.COM

"In *Facing the Sunshine,* Sara Jane Thornton explores her psychological journey from victim of sexual abuse, through depression and anorexia, to recovery and becoming a survivor. In her courageous story she shares the pain and horror, the progress and regressions, she experienced through the course of years of treatment. Readers will develop a deeper understanding of the cognitive state of anorexics, the application of their intelligence to the goal of starving themselves, and the value of positive reinforcement and empathy in their treatment. Sara also shares the many ways she struggled with care-givers and the challenges that professionals can expect to experience when working with patients with severe eating disorders. For these reasons alone, Facing the Sunshine is an invaluable resource for such professionals."

—DAVID HIRSHBERG, EDD
EXECUTIVE DIRECTOR, GERMAINE LAWRENCE SCHOOL
ARLINGTON, MASSACHUSETTS


"Thornton's is a journey of courage and hope; her message, vitally, one of compassion. She shines a light on the catastrophic consequences not only of sexual abuse but also of inept therapeutic intervention. Thornton's ultimate recovery with the help of skilled and empathic therapists proves the critical need for a revision of standards to ensure more humane and effective psychiatric care."

—AIMEE LIU
AUTHOR OF *GAINING: THE TRUTH ABOUT LIFE AFTER EATING DISORDERS*


"Although Sara's story is startling with her frank description of a chaotic life, it is a sadly common fate to sufferers of childhood sexual abuse. Sara speaks for multitudes of women and men who have been victimized, and in turn have dysfunctional relationships, eating disorders, substance abuse, and self-mutilation, and other symptoms of borderline personality disorder. Her depiction of the insidious nature of anorexia nervosa is graphic and offers a clear picture of this life-threatening eating disorder."

—LEIGH COHN, MAT, CEDS
EDITOR-IN-CHIEF, *EATING DISORDERS:*
*THE JOURNAL OF TREATMENT AND PREVENTION*

"This story raises important questions about the treatment of the mentally ill and highlights grave deficiencies in the medical community, while leading us along a path of suffering, perseverance, and finally, recovery."

—MELISSA R. GERSON, LMSW
PSYCHOTHERAPIST AND EATING DISORDERS SPECIALIST

"As we sail through life, we are met with events, people, or lessons that cause us to stop and reflect on our own life, the world around us, and who we are. As we get older, the lessons we learn have a harder time impacting our lives. Sara's book twists the events of my life into a reality that I only can trust to Sara's words, feelings, and struggles. How insignificant my trials and tribulations; by the first third of her book, I was searching for understanding and meaning that I could only get from her pain and suffering that she shared so honestly. I am at a loss that someone has to experience such events to teach us such a valuable lesson of perseverance once again."

—ERNEST CAMPAGNONE, EdD
ADJUNCT PROFESSOR, HUMAN SERVICES,
COMMUNITY COLLEGE OF RHODE ISLAND

# Facing the Sunshine

*"Once in a while you get shown the light
in the strangest of places
if you look at it right."*

—Jerry Garcia

# Facing the Sunshine

## A Young Woman's Emergence from the
## Shadows of Sexual Abuse and Anorexia

# SARA JANE THORNTON

### Foreword by Beverly Engel

SOARING
WINGS
PRESS

Salem, New Hampshire

*Published by:*

Soaring Wings Press
A Division of Appelstein Training Resources, LLC
12 Martin Avenue
Salem, NH 03079


Editor: Ellen Kleiner

Conceptual and clinical consultant: Charles Appelstein, MSW

Design and production: Angela Werneke

**Publisher's Cataloging-in-Publication Data**

Thornton, Sara Jane.

Facing the sunshine : a young woman's emergence from the shadows of sexual
   abuse and anorexia / Sara Jane Thornton. -- 1st ed. -- Salem, N.H. : Soaring
Wings Press, 2007.

   p. ; cm.

   ISBN-13: 978-0-9763694-6-2
   ISBN-10: 0-9763694-6-X
   Includes bibliographical references.

   1. Thornton, Sara Jane. 2. Adult child sexual abuse victims--Psychology.
   3. Adult child sexual abuse victims--Biography. 4. Anorexia nervosa--
   Patients--Psychology. 5. Sexual abuse victims' writings. 6. Anorexia nervosa
   patients' writings. I. Title.

RC560.S44 T46 2007                                              2007923240
616.85/83690651--dc22                                           0710


10   9   8   7   6   5   4   3   2   1

*To the millions of people grappling with mental disorders ~*
*As you face the darkest and most turbulent days,*
*have faith that the sun shall shine again,*
*since it cannot rain forever.*

# Acknowledgments

The creation of this book has become a grand story within a story, filled with noble spirits I think of as my angels, for they have impacted my life in profound ways. I shall be forever grateful to each one of them:

Charlie Appelstein, for renewing my belief that any goal is possible and reminding me of the infinite potential within us all. No words can express the gratitude I feel for your leap of faith in publishing this book. You have not only opened the door with a miracle but walked through it offering friendship. I thank your lovely family as well, for embracing your decision to embark on this voyage.

Ellen Kleiner, for living far beyond the expectations of an editor while adding clarity and brilliance to this work. I am in awe of your talent, mastery with words, patience, and humor, all of which have made this an immensely joyous experience. By way of your insight and passion, my love for writing has only flourished.

Angela Werneke, for an abundance of creative contributions, from book design to artistic visual imagery inside and out. The cover captures my vision perfectly.

Doug Church, for creating facingthesunshine.com, where I can connect with this book's readers and offer essential resources. I thank you for your friendship and enthusiasm. You're a rare gem.

I am also forever grateful to the many individuals who have given life to my soul:

To the psychologists, social workers, occupational therapists, dietitians, pharmacists, psychiatric nurses, and attendants who provided a foundation from which I could grow.

To my fellow patients, the true inspiration behind this book, whose exceptional strength and bravery awakened within me a passion for patient advocacy.

To my former weight trainer, who invariably found me with

not a single reason to continue fighting and left me with ten.

To my former employers and coworkers, whose respect and sensitivity created accepting environments free of prejudice.

To the members of my community, distant relatives, and childhood friends, whose outreach infused me with courage.

To Amie Churchill, who from the very beginning rode this rollercoaster with grace, often holding my hand through fearful times.

To my mother, for staying by my side and reminding me that I am fully equipped to follow my heart.

To my brother, my knight in shining armor, who predicted my promising destiny and taught me the truth of unconditional love.

To my sister, for remaining proud of me and defending my honor despite my behavior to the contrary.

To my father, for inadvertently teaching me to accept the consequences of my actions and face life's challenges, no matter how intense the circumstances may appear to be.

To Christopher, who has imbued me with trust, confidence, and the luxury of time to bring this book to completion. I thank you for your friendship on this journey through life.

And to our daughter, Fallon, for continually mirroring back a new future.

# Publisher's Note

$W$hen I first read Sara's manuscript, it hurt so much that I could read only a chapter at a time. Somehow I could feel her pain, despair, and occasional desire to die. I was also terribly frustrated. At times she would profess hope for herself, and I'd buy it. I'd get excited that the agony she had so eloquently described—and I had experienced with her—was over. But a few sentences later, she'd be hurting herself again, with no explanation for the sudden change. At other times she would refer briefly to her father, the man who sexually abused her, and I'd want to hear more so I could better understand her circumstances, but nothing more would follow. Yet the more I read, the more I realized how exquisitely authentic her words were. She was writing to survive, not sell books. And she was walking us through her ordeal in a way that few guides ever accomplish.

As a person interested in human capabilities, I felt honored to be let into her world. And as a youth care specialist, I knew Sara's story would inspire confidence in people dealing with abuse and anorexia. It is, after all, about our intrinsic capacity to rise above the ashes of despair when the treatment we receive is humane and supportive of our strengths.

So I decided to publish *Facing the Sunshine,* knowing some of the missing pieces and mood swings would need to be addressed to help the book achieve its goal of bringing light and warmth. I think the current edition does that. The editor, while capturing the raw emotion of Sara's experience, has also encouraged her to fill in the pieces. The result is an intimate glimpse into a fractured life that has since healed.

# Contents

# Foreword

Survivor stories such as *Facing the Sunshine* are important to tell. One reason is that child sexual abuse proves to be such a devastating assault against mind, body, and soul, affecting every facet of an individual's existence—among them, self-esteem, ability to trust, physical and emotional health, sexuality, achievement, and interpersonal relationships—that survivors need to know they are not alone. *Facing the Sunshine* offers them this understanding, as well as the strength and will to continue their recovery. The key to beginning their recovery, on the other hand, is to rob the abuse of its power, which Sara Jane Thornton demonstrates by bringing her experiences out in the open. With the added benefit of perspective and insight, she frees her spirit of emotional toxins and shame.

Survivor stories are important for those who have not been abused, as well. Family members, partners, and close friends of individuals who were sexually traumatized need to understand how the abuse affected their loved one. In learning about what the person endured, it becomes possible to stop judging and start empathizing, and to realize how the abuse resulted in acting-out behaviors—such as promiscuity, self-destructiveness, over-control and abuse of others, stealing, addictions, attraction to abusive partners, and, in the case of Sara and many other survivors, eating disorders.

Professionals, too, can gain from reading true life accounts such as Sara's. Having worked with child sexual abuse survivors for more than thirty years, I can honestly say I have learned more from them than through school or training programs. Consistently, these clients open doors to how they think, feel, and most importantly, what they need.

Above all, the public needs to read accounts such as *Facing the Sunshine*. Despite the growing number of educational and recovery programs now available, child sexual abuse remains the most hidden and ignored form of abuse, and one still marked by stigma and shame. In the United States, where as many as 25 percent of all girls and 16 percent of all boys are known to have been sexually abused, the public remains in denial about how rampant this behavior is. We prefer to believe that child molesters are the "perverted monsters" we hear about on the news—not the parents, grandparents, siblings, and other relatives who smile sweetly and dispense hugs. Stories like Sara's bring awareness of abuse home, where it most often occurs.

Every survivor's story is different and yet very much the same, in terms of being a source of fear, pain, humiliation, and shame. Some project these emotions in outbursts of rage; others carry them inwardly, wrestling with depression throughout their adult lives. These and other effects of child sexual abuse cannot be erased, but they can be diminished and coped with in a healthy way. For survivors with the courage to admit past sexual abuse, talk about the damage, and work it through, there is hope.

There is also help. The luckiest survivors can engage in professional therapy with a competent, compassionate expert in sexual abuse recovery. For survivors unable to afford this option, sexual abuse recovery centers and rape crisis centers throughout North America offer affordable, and often free, support groups and peer counseling. Connecting with other survivors, hearing their stories, and feeling consistently supported can be immensely healing, as can advice offered in self-help books on recovery.

Healing from child sexual abuse may also arise when survivors are left alone with their thoughts and feelings. Deep inner work—which may entail journaling, grieving, releasing anger and pain, or otherwise allowing the tears to flow freely—takes tremendous fortitude. In fact, I have never known a group of people as courageous and resilient as survivors of child sexual abuse.

Sara Jane Thornton is a shining example of the inner strength and determination it takes to become whole again. Even though she was helped by many people, including some she became angry with, it was because of her courage, perseverance, and dedication to recovery that she has not only healed but, in writing this book, contributed instrumentally to the healing of others.

—Beverly Engel, MFT
Diplomat American Psychotherapy Association
Author of *The Right to Innocence*

# Preface

*L*ittle did I realize at age six that pushing my bed against the door at night and pleading not to be sent on father-daughter trips on weekends reflected an instinctive fight for survival. Nor did I imagine the battle, enshrouded in clouds of darkness, would rage on after the midnight visits finally ended, six long years later. But it did.

*Facing the Sunshine* is a true account of a journey to well-being following a childhood lost in the shadows of sexual abuse and subsequent mental illness. The journey began with the arduous retrieval of traumatic experiences, an ordeal that tested me, for I had buried some in places far from my consciousness. The more of them I unearthed, however, the better equipped I became to understand my inner self. Fortified by these insights, I eventually came to terms with my menacing past so I could heal. But it was in writing about my recovery—not only from the childhood sexual abuse but from the ensuing struggle with everything from obsessive-compulsive disorder and anorexia nervosa to suicide attempts—that I found meaning in my past, which enabled me to reconnect with the boundless spirit I once possessed.

While this book explores my personal winding path to self-awareness and recovery as a foundation for future wellness, it is also about the amazing survival instinct and potential we all have for healing. And whereas some segments may be offensive to the reader, the purpose of including explicit descriptions of my experiences is to inspire, challenge, and educate individuals suffering from such disorders, as well as those assisting in the healing.

I am very grateful for the many people who influenced my life and those who encouraged me to write about it in this book. Although it is based on actual events and individuals, their names have been changed to protect their privacy. I have decided not to protect my father, however; nor do I wish to shame him or cause my family to suffer as a result of public disclosure of private experiences, but only to reveal the elements necessary for healing to occur. For me to make sense of my childhood misery, it had to have a purpose. Similarly, in sharing my past through the writing of this book, I hope to shape a new future.

To best express the various facets of my healing, the book alternates between present insights and excerpts from journals written during my participation in a variety of treatments. As such, it presents the entire evolution of my disorders as well as my fears and eventual insights about recovering. They will have more than served their purpose if these experiences help the reader better understand others who have suffered the agony of abuse and, perhaps more importantly, assist them in anticipating an infinitely brighter future.

# Introduction

*I* decided in September of 2000, at age twenty-four, to come back to my childhood home, the place where my problems began, to make it the place where they would finally end. My intent was to undergo a symbolic suicide and rebirth—to quickly close what I considered to be a sad and forgettable chapter of my life and start anew, only to learn that this chapter was in fact still being composed. In retrospect, I realize that I was drawn back to my childhood home to resolve the conflicts that still plagued my troubled body, mind, and soul.

As it turned out, I stayed for two years, living under the same roof with my father, who had sexually abused me as recently as twelve years before. My mother, older brother, and older sister had by then moved out, so the sole occupants were my father and myself. During my first one hundred days at home I compiled this book, interweaving accounts of my time there with journal entries I'd made during my previous two years of hospital treatment. Subsequently I attended college and exorcised a few demons. In addition, I transformed the basement of the house, applying fresh paint that I now know will never obliterate my dismal memories of the place. I didn't touch the upper half of the house, however. It remains as if time stood still—with its 1970s shag carpet, the smell of mothballs on my dead grandmother's furniture, and the curtains my mother hung while she was pregnant with me.

My father now lives alone in this house. In fact, it occurs to me that maybe he was alone when we all lived there together. He struggles often with the realization that he sexually abused me, alternating between expressing remorse, accountability, and a desire to understand his past actions. He also clings tenaciously to a memory of my childhood as innocent and joyful. It is no coincidence that my room has been restored to look as it did then, with small twin beds, Girl Scout uniforms hanging in the closet, and propped in the corner, two teddy bears that comforted me in the menacing hours after midnight.

While my father admits to having blocks about the past, I have not been as fortunate. I remember what he did to me in the shower, under his covers, and on the plaid couch in the basement. I also recall the recurring game of "hot dog." It is little wonder, then, that writing this book in the solitude of my father's basement ignited a flood of emotions. Being home literally and figuratively, I subsequently felt a wheel of health and absolution in ceaseless motion, initiating waves of catharsis.

The chapters that follow, arranged chronologically during those first one hundred days in my father's house, juxtapose my unexpected experiences there with a chronicle of my fractured life as I knew it until that time. The first four chapters address the horrors leading to the demise of my childhood and adolescence, which ultimately yielded symptoms of anorexia nervosa, a debilitating eating disorder. The next six chapters describe the controversial, and often adverse, treatment I underwent at the hands of a pedantic and regimented physician on staff at the local hospital. Chapter 11 examines the challenges I faced as a result of leaving treatment prematurely. Chapter 12 portrays the mismanagement I suffered upon being readmitted on involuntary status, after which I was transferred to a facility approximately two hours from my hometown. Chapters 13 and 14 chronicle the more self-empowering treatment I received at this facility, where I spent time as both an involuntary and voluntary patient. Chapters 15 and 16 elucidate a thwarted attempt to reclaim my freedom and well-being while living independently. Finally, in Chapter 17 the past merges with the present, allowing me to embrace the moment while finding purpose in those that came before.

To avoid propagating the textbook mentality that guided a significant portion of my four years of treatment, it must be pointed out that my experience with anorexia cannot justifiably be generalized to that of others. Although common threads and related symptoms unite anorexia sufferers, we are more than our diagnosis and self-destructive behaviors. We are each an individual on a path of our own, lit continually by the guiding spirit of love, no matter how dark the night may seem. In the end, it was the enormous constellation of love in my midst that saved my life and taught me how to love myself. For when I faced the sunshine the shadows fell behind.

## CHAPTER ONE

# Coming Home

*D*ay 1: Today, September 13, 2000, I returned to the haunting house where I grew up, moving in with my father, who sexually abused me as a child and made my life a living hell. As I confront the painful events of my early years, I hope to learn how to let go of the past so I can find my purpose in life and ultimately fulfill my potential.

Coming back to this place in New Brunswick, Canada, where the abuse occurred is already triggering horrendous memories of hearing my father's footsteps on the stairs, running my hands along the tiles in his shower, and staring at the ceiling from my childhood bed. Perhaps if I surrender to the memories instead of running from them, they will stop chasing me and ultimately lose the power I have endowed them with over the past nine years. This task seems daunting but necessary for my inner freedom and peace.

As I stretch out on a sofa in the basement, where the old plaid hideaway bed used to be, I'm hardly surprised that my father has not yet come home from work, and I welcome the opportunity to reflect on my childhood in this typically middle-class neighborhood where each house rested comfortably on its one-acre plot and every second floor contained a Block Parent sign. It was, and still is, the kind of neighborhood where one might expect to find a white picket fence around every house. During the days, the children played hopscotch in the streets without fear of danger, retiring at night to the surrounding forest for a game of truth or dare. We were semiprivileged children with dreams of adventure and parents who rigorously maintained the neighborhood's pleasing appearance. The men kept the lawns neatly trimmed, while the women meticulously pruned the gardens. My parents followed suit, so impeccably that the neighbors had no idea there lived amongst them a child molester—a truth that remains untold to this day.

In contrast to its serene exterior, the setting in which I was raised felt far from idyllic. My home offered little comfort and no routines to soothe the wounded soul. Fortunately I managed to seek refuge elsewhere. As a child I was considered pretty, athletic, and popular among my peers; as a teenager, despite often outrageous behavior, I was invited to the most exclusive functions and my weekends were usually booked well in advance.

In effect, the tapestry of my youth resembled a patchwork quilt made up of clashing fabrics that continually unraveled at the seams. In particular, while I remained free of peer pressure and other stressors that typically plague adolescents, the surface perfection of my life hid a marred core. Between the ages of six and eighteen, I lived in darkness, abused and neglected on many levels. For years my mother, a victim of depression, spent hours each day holed up in the laundry room, either sleeping or reading novels by Danielle Steele to escape her misery, while my father, a high-profile engineer well respected by his colleagues, was sexually abusing me in the basement at night.

My mother hadn't always suffered from depression. The eldest of four children raised by a doting mother and hard-working father in a middle-class home, she excelled at field hockey and basketball in her youth and graduated from Dalhousie University with a degree in physiotherapy, whereupon she married my father. As a very young child, I delighted at my mother's effervescent laughter and enthusiasm for life. She was nurturing and tender, and every meal she prepared showed up drizzled with love.

My mother's cheerful disposition did not endure the test of time perhaps because my father's deceptions were her first exposure to such prodigious dishonesty and corruption. Whatever the cause, she soon walled herself off from family life, especially interactions with my father. Then, just as a flower withers with age, so did my mother's expressions of affection. Although for a while I would catch her being vivacious out in public, in the privacy of our home she would turn lifeless.

It was painful to stand by helplessly as my mother slipped deeper into the throes of depression while her relationship with my father crumbled. Despite her declining mental health, however, she eventually opened her own physio-therapy business and separated from my father, inviting me to come live with her. At sixteen and lacking structure, I accepted the offer, hungry for whatever guidance I might be able to siphon from our deteriorating relationship.

Unlike my mother's background, my father's raises more questions than it answers. He was brought up on a farm by his mother and uncles, one of whom was a mute hermit whose stares passed chillingly through me the day I met him. The departure of my father's father was never discussed and remained unaddressed throughout my childhood. I am told that my father was an exceptionally sociable and intelligent student at the local university, and that after consuming alcohol he would become overbearing and obnox-ious, dancing with a lampshade on his head and generally making a fool of himself.

Other than his dominant genes for a darker-than-average complexion and full lips, and his openhandedness with money, my father shared very lit-tle of himself with his children. He would immerse himself in his work, spend-ing long hours at the office or away on business matters. Upon his return home, he was often critical and verbally abusive toward my mother and con-trolling and physically threatening toward my two older siblings and myself.

In the 1980s, I am told, his behavior became unusually obscure. During moments of heightened paranoia, when he wasn't hiding mysterious documents, he would insist the curtains in our home remain closed. Although he has never been diagnosed, it appears he might suffer from obsessive-compulsive disorder, for he'd often become fixated on things to the point of being unable to let go of his perseverative thinking and accompanying behaviors. I recall a time when my father was so consumed by a fear of AIDS that he restlessly left newspaper clippings about it on our bedroom doors and constantly preached that tattoos and premarital sex would inevitably lead to its precursor, HIV.

It was during these years that my father forced me to endure the humil-iation and torture of molestation. But not until I was in the safe confines of a hospital eleven years later did I finally confront him. By then he was not the same man but rather gentle and mild tempered, a change in disposition perhaps marking an acceptance of what he had done to me and his family. Although he initially denied my accusations of sexual abuse, whereupon I refused to talk with him for an entire year, his memories of the abuse eventually surfaced and he sought treatment for a dissociative disorder. After receiving letters from my father in which he pleaded for forgiveness for his violent actions, I eventually invited him into my life and requested permission to move into his home for purposes of my own healing—which is why I am here now.

Already, three things have become clear: I love my mom and dad, I harbor other feelings for them as well, and that's okay.

Whereas most girls look up to their daddies, I idolized my brother Lance, who, five years my senior, insisted that I walk by his side. Emotionally sensitive and unafraid to express his feelings for others, Lance taught me the meaning of unconditional love. During my childhood, he was my hero and savior; when I became consumed by illness as a young adult, he resumed these roles with even more intelligence, insight, and uncanny wisdom.

My sister Jackie, born almost exactly one year after Lance, set standards for me, as well. Jackie sometimes joked that I was the milkman's daughter, and went so far as to tell me the doctor had dropped me as an infant, which explained why I lack the prominent nose that she and Lance possess. Never one to tolerate cruelty, she routinely defended my honor in public places. And while our relationship has been strained at times by occasional differences of opinion, she exhibits qualities I have longed to attain, such as an ability to remain composed while under great stress.

I, on the other hand, am overtly expressive and invite drama. As an infant and toddler, however, I was content and joyous, or so I am told. My placid temperament began turning explosive around age six, mirroring the confusion I experienced over my father's treatment of me. Unable to relate to the highly sensitive child I had become, my parents resorted to frequent punishment—my mother by way of spanking and verbal reprimands, and my father through threats of physical violence—and ultimately, planned neglect. In elementary school, I turned to humor as a coping mechanism and took pride in making others laugh, usually at my own expense though sometimes at that of innocent bystanders.

For me, menstruation—which most girls regarded as a curse—came as a blessing since it marked the end of my sexual abuse, though at the time, my memories of the abuse were blocked and I had concluded that my father was rejecting me. In response, I began to relate to men very differently. At school, although I earned academic honors, my teachers regularly sent me to the guidance counselor for having issues with male authority figures. One day the principal called my mother in for a meeting to inquire about my behavior toward my father. In typical fashion, my mother defended me and the family. Yet in my mind I was sure she recalled the spell of terror this man had cast over us, images of me hiding behind her as my father shook his fist and curled the side of his lip, of how I never embraced him when he returned from a business trip and in fact rejoiced each time he left, and the intense anger I felt toward this man even when I wasn't announcing my hatred for him. Lastly, I was sure she remembered the tears streaming down my face every time I pleaded with her to leave him and take me with her. Though my mother knew my attitude toward my father was not in any way typical, I don't think she was capable of dealing with it at the time, for her own demons were madly wreaking havoc on her psyche.

During this difficult phase of my life, it wasn't only male authority figures I rebelled against but anyone who tried to influence me. I was so out of control that I would burst into tears for no apparent reason and even threatened my mother with a knife. Finally, in addition to daily crying spells and outbursts of anger, I started to abuse alcohol, engage in promiscuous behavior with the neighborhood high school boys, and practice self-mutilation (cutting). No one intervened to stop me. I surmise that my parents and teachers either saw these behaviors as characteristic of adolescence or had already written me off as a lost cause.

By the time I entered middle school, I had displaced my inner insecurity onto outer phenomena. At first, I strove for physical beauty through hair dye, makeup, and designer clothing. I was convinced that in coming to peace with my appearance I would be fully capable of squelching the turmoil that churned in the pit of my stomach day and night. So dedicated was I to hiding behind physical accessories that I had no idea my appearance—at 5 feet 3 inches tall and 115 pounds, with green eyes, button nose, and shoulder-length blonde hair—did not begin to measure up to that of the sophisticated women whose images graced the covers of the magazines I intently studied.

As my family life continued to deteriorate, I turned to athletics, figuring that if I couldn't achieve inner satisfaction by looking great perhaps I could assuage my inner pain by finding greatness on the playing field. But ironically, I had long before exchanged my team affiliation for camaraderie with a crowd that accepted my alcohol and drug use and refrained from overtly judging my increasingly promiscuous conduct.

Despite my extremely problematic behaviors and underlying angst, I nevertheless began high school as if it were the start of a new era. My ecstatic feelings about life were rooted in the fact that I had a dreamy boyfriend, Justin, who had chosen me above the fifteen hundred other girls at our high school. A popular senior and star quarterback for the football team, Justin was my first love.

Meanwhile my father, though no longer sexually abusive, had become more physically abusive. One night he caught me sneaking out of the house with a pint of gin and threw me against the fridge in a mad rage before I managed to escape to the local Burger King with my friend Terry. At around 10:00 p.m., a hockey player drove up, told me his parents were away, and invited me to spend the night. Once there I went immediately to sleep, but when Justin found out that I had slept at this guy's house, he assumed the worst. Rather than telling Justin the truth, however, I proceeded to make myself look guilty, subconsciously initiating a breakup with him. Although I loved him dearly, I thought that if he ever found out what I was really like he would no longer love me. Before long, I had established a pattern soon to become deeply entrenched: rejecting those I loved before they could reject me. It wasn't until much later that I perceived how problematic this pattern could be.

The rest of my freshman year is a blur of rebellious behavior, involving parties, binge drinking, marijuana, a trip to the drunk-tank, and a few to the local hospital following alcohol poisoning. Although I still considered myself a good athlete, I was in no shape to participate in sports—hell, I was having enough trouble participating in life. At this point, my mother left my father, taking me with her. Grateful to be out of the house, I went back one last time to throw a house-destroying party.

During my sophomore year, the anger turned to rage, directed mostly at my mother. No doubt I blamed her for not protecting me from childhood sexual abuse, but I also did not like the fact that she was becoming independent and self-confident instead of the depressed and introverted person I'd grown accustomed to. In addition to her physiotherapy business and apartment of her own, she now had a new best friend, Janice, whom I viewed as competition for her affections. Rocked by uncertainty and instability, I lashed out at them constantly. Before long my violent outbursts, combined with my generally unpredictable demeanor—informed by the years of abuse and lack of parental protection—had developed into such an overwhelming burden that my mother asked me to leave.

Freedom at age sixteen carried a stiff price, especially for someone already headed down a spiral of self-destruction.

## CHAPTER TWO

# INTO THE MAELSTROM

*Day 3:* Despite a newly laid beige carpet, fresh coat of white paint, and a wooden door my father recently hung to separate my temporary quarters down here from the rest of the house, the basement reeks of mildew and the cloying dampness of melancholy, as if compelled to diffuse the evil it once held. Nevertheless, I feel an unusual sense of relief to be back in this place of madness, for I know that if I fail to confront the past it will chase me forever.

Oddly, in the three days I have been living in my father's house our paths have crossed on only rare occasions. He still works long days, then after returning home he stops by briefly with a submarine sandwich for me. When I hear him at the door to my apartment, I briefly unlock it and slide my hand out to receive the sandwich. He then mutters, "I'm terribly sorry, Sara," at which point I close the door, unwilling to discuss the abuse in the very location it occurred. As his footsteps recede up the stairs, I eat the offering and withdraw emotionally back into the dank stillness of the room. At times my grief is so overwhelming that I weep loudly, if only to break the silence.

An old family photograph on the wall reminds me of the shift that occurred in my relationship with my father after I left my mother's house.

Now *I* was the one with all the control, causing him to be cautious and overly generous toward me—behavior that may have been fueled by guilt, or perhaps a subconscious desire to buy my silence. In any case, I decided to use against him the very strategy he had used with me: manipulation.

Aware that he was obsessed with education and careers leading to status and wealth, I told him that since I had nowhere to live, I would have to quit school and find full-time employment to provide for myself. To drive the point home, I added that living with him wasn't an option because his house was deteriorating and essentially uninhabitable.

This maneuver worked like a charm: I got to stay in school and make high marks; he, for his part, bought me a car, paid rent on an apartment for me, provided me with a weekly income, and took me and my friends on vacation during the holidays. And despite his financial chivalry, I was extremely mean to him, refusing to let him dodge my verbal abuse just as he had not allowed me to escape his sexual abuse. He had to put up with my behavior or be exposed, losing everything he had worked his entire life to build—his reputation, successful career, and confidentiality. Clearly it was my turn to be the abuser.

At the beginning of my junior year of high school, my behavior toward my father began showing up in actions toward boys my own age. Come September, I had a new love named Sam, who was handsome, a real gentleman, and star of the high school hockey team. Eventually Sam moved in with me, getting more than he bargained for, or deserved. I had ambivalent feelings toward men, both loving and hating them, and unfortunately Sam became a target of my anger. Not only was I unfaithful to him, I was both verbally and physically abusive whenever trigger events arose reminding me of my father. And viewing life through the eyes of a victim, I did not see how inappropriate my behavior had become. While my disturbed childhood was surely the culprit, it was no excuse for mistreating Sam—or, as it turned out, myself.

Flooded with thoughts of suicide and fierce mood swings, fluctuating from euphoria to intense anger to deep sadness, I knew it was time to get help. My mother had already determined that I needed counseling. For her the clincher was when I pulled a door off its hinges and days later punched a hole in the hallway wall. Consequently, she took me to a counselor she had been seeing named Sally, with whom I felt an immediate connection. Following one of my earliest visits, Sally shocked my mother by commenting during one of their private sessions, "Your daughter sounds like she's been sexually abused."

My own realization of the abuse came from memories triggered by Sally's questions about my first sexual experiences. In response to her inquiries, I desperately wanted to say my first sexual encounter was with Justin, but I knew in my heart that was not so. Right away, secrets from my middle-school years flooded back at me in a rush of memories. While the other girls were having slumber parties, I was sneaking out of the house to meet high school boys from the neighborhood, get drunk, and perform degrading sexual acts for them. I recalled, for example, at age twelve giving oral sex to a boy in a crawl space and, despite my reluctance, thinking that saying no was not an option. As I related this story to Sally, something became terrifyingly clear: I had performed the act like a pro. Then tears came to my eyes and I said despairingly, *"I knew exactly how to do it … because my father used to force me to do it to him."*

I couldn't remember exactly when my father began molesting me, though I strongly suspected it was during my sixth year of life. It ended, I recalled, when I started menstruating at age twelve. The abuse consisted mostly of oral sex and mutual touching. In my father's invented game of hot dog, for example, I was the hot dog and he would pretend to put mustard, ketchup, and relish on me, touching me all over until focusing his attention on my genital region.

The more I talked with Sally, the further I slipped into the past as ever-new images of abuse consumed my waking thoughts, arriving in surreal pictures and hurtling me into an altered reality. Suddenly I would be a terrorized six-year-old lying in bed at night, aware that her siblings were fast asleep and her mother was working late at the local hospital. Hearing the eerie creaking of the wooden stairs, I would grip the blankets tightly, praying that my father would reach the second-floor landing and walk past my room. But always the door would open and I would be summoned to the basement, where he would pull out the hideaway bed, press my head under the covers, and guide my hand up and down his body.

Or I would morph into a seven-year-old awakening from a nightmare. Padding into my parents' bedroom, I would curl up next to my mother and grit my teeth to avoid confiding my intense fear to her. How I wanted her to know that no nightmare was as scary as the acts my father had been subjecting me to while she slept silently next to him.

Sometimes I was a ten-year-old choking on a mouthful of water as my father forced my lips around his penis in the shower. At other times I'd feel an obscure sense of relief, aware retrospectively that I was swept up in a final sexual encounter with my father that took place during a visit to his mother's apartment. Seeing in my mind the butterfly-shaped anti-skid stickers that lined her bathtub both made me cringe and reminded me that I too would soon fly free of the constraints that enveloped me.

Sally informed me that these episodes and others were signs of post-traumatic stress disorder (PTSD), a reaction involving daydreams, memories, or flashbacks of extremely upsetting events, triggered by various sensory cues, including scents, tastes, sights, and spoken words. My most disturbing flashbacks, I knew, were triggered by being touched during moments of intimacy. In response to any sensation that reminded me of the sexual abuse, I would become violent, displacing my anger onto an innocent partner. So confused was I by these negative thoughts associated with intimacy that I began to question my sexuality and core sense of being.

The PTSD cost me more as well. Disoriented and highly anxious, I missed so many days of school that my teachers petitioned to have me expelled for the remainder of the year. When I met with the vice principal, I at last disclosed that classes had become challenging because I was being treated for PTSD stemming from childhood sexual abuse. He replied that I was "wound up tighter than a clock" and could continue my education, if I wished, in school detention, performing cafeteria duty every lunch hour. Humiliated, I officially quit school, determined to decide for myself the best course for the future.

That summer I spent two weeks visiting a quaint village in Quebec to be with my brother Lance, in an effort to clear my mind, get an infusion of positive energy, and decide on a path to follow. But first, to enhance my approval ratings I had my long streaked-blonde hair cut to a pixie style and colored platinum. I also traded in my designer wardrobe for plaid flannel shirts and Doc Martin combat boots. While secretly fearing that a villager might consider me an imposter and sentence me to a horrid fate reserved for outcasts, I also knew Lance didn't care what I wore or what point of view I subscribed to; he welcomed my individuality. Perhaps that is why I was less judgmental upon meeting the villagers, and in fact more open-minded than ever before. Rarely did I label them, for the imaginary line separating myself from others had begun to fade. The importance I had long placed on how people looked or what they did in the world, paled in comparison to their humor or kindness or some other human attribute. Perhaps the most lasting change that occurred during my time with Lance emerged from a card he handed me, in which he had written, *"Different* is not a bad word, Sara."* This message inspired me to stop fearing rejection and to realize that if Lance could embrace my eccentricity others would as well.

Returning to New Brunswick with my new grunge look and confident attitude, I glanced out the train window and saw Sam waving excitedly. I then flashed on our turbulent relationship and knew without a doubt that I needed to change not only my thinking and appearance, but how I wanted to live my life. And sure enough, by the end of the summer I had dissolved my relationship with Sam, reenrolled in high school, and committed to focusing on my studies so I could someday attend a university and strive to fulfill my potential. I had terminated my sessions with Sally, too, in part to avoid disappointing her in the event that no more memories would surface, but mostly to stop thinking of the sexual abuse in the hope that my memories of it would then vanish.

Intent on forging new bonds, I soon acquired a best friend, Anna. First, however, I had to suffer through weeks of knowing my secrets were being exposed by old friends who now spoke freely about my mood swings, outbursts of anger, and promiscuity. Because people did not know the underlying causes for such behavior—namely, sexual abuse and the PTSD that came in its wake—I felt isolated and misunderstood. Worse, as time passed Anna and I were labeled lesbians. "Coming out of the closet" during high school would have been difficult enough, but I had to endure the stigma of being gay though I was not, and also of contradictory rumors claiming I was a slut.

Around this time, I moved out of the one-room apartment I had shared with Sam and into a two-bedroom apartment with Kathy, a new friend who had graduated from high school the year before and was kind of wild. I soon started living a double life: as a seventeen-year-old high school student by day and a nineteen-year-old club kid at night. I spent the first six months of my senior year of high school dropping LSD, smoking marijuana, going to bars on school nights, and being highly promiscuous. I was a free agent—until I met Anthony and once again fell in love.

Anthony was much different from my earlier flames. He matched me almost perfectly in height and weight and, projecting an air of confidence and daring, was an extremist in all that he did, including motorbiking, mountain climbing, and especially skiing. As such, he provided the excitement I yearned for like a drug—a discovery that should have forewarned me about trouble ahead.

As friends we were like two peas in a pod, but as intimate partners we became increasingly like oil and water the more that sexual tension and jealousy plagued our relationship. On our first date, Anthony spent the night, and from then on we never went to bed without each other; in fact, he soon moved in with me and Kathy. His buddies, all of whom had matching tattoos and would have died for one another, were often up to no good, though they weren't exactly a gang since they were free to be uniquely themselves. Although upset by the violence that occurred when their values clashed with those of others, I felt safe nestled in the strength of their numbers. And they, for their part, accepted me as part of the group, calling me Steve, as if I were one of them. For the first time in my life I felt worthy of being protected.

Although I initially thought my PTSD symptoms had subsided and that with Anthony I would finally be able to have a healthy, constructive relationship, the dreaded symptoms returned in connection with intimacy. As long as I was intoxicated, I could suppress the terrifying feelings and dissociate from sexual acts—a skill I had learned at a young age during incidents with my father. But I was unable to stop myself from verbally and physically abusing Anthony. Often our arguments accelerated into either high-speed car chases or physical fights during which I would punch and kick him while he aggressively restrained me through hair-pulling and pushing. Usually we fought because we were jealous by nature; at other times, it was because I sought to disobey him since I wanted to control, and not be controlled.

After receiving a promise ring from Anthony and spending a romantic summer together camping, I sabotaged the relationship by sleeping with a guy named Peter, with whom I had been infatuated. A week later, Anthony asked me if there was a future for us and, learning that there wasn't, decided to move to Canada's West Coast to pursue his dream of becoming an extreme skier. While gathering one night with a group of friends to send him off, I had strong misgivings, certain that no one would ever accept me—for both my strengths and weaknesses—as Anthony had.

Peter and I were a short-lived item that revolved around sex and romantic gestures rather than love and honesty. Missing Anthony increasingly as my senior year unfolded, I decided to fly west during Christmas break and win back his heart—a mission propelled also by envy for his love of skiing and his sense of purpose and competence. Anthony returned home with me, whereupon I went out of control even more. This time I was unable to stabilize my mood swings, my PTSD flared up, and exams were approaching, causing me extreme stress that ultimately spiraled into a breakdown.

One night I wandered into the nearby woods in a state of anxiety, became lost, developed hypothermia, and landed in the emergency room, preoccupied with suicidal thoughts. Anthony called my mother who, together with the ER staff, decided I needed to resume therapy with Sally. Anthony supported the idea and even attended a few sessions with me, asking Sally how he could help and assuring me we would get through the crisis together. But this time my work with her was even more fleeting than before, undermined by my determination to suppress all feelings and thoughts associated with the sexual abuse and to find wellness in averting my innermost demons.

My family doctor, believing I needed medication, referred me to a psychiatrist named Dr. Black. He was handsome and warm, and I loved him immediately though I couldn't figure out if these were feelings driven by sexual attraction or adoration for a father figure. In any case, Dr. Black prescribed a six-month supply of antidepressants—a solution I welcomed. And aware that my dream of attending a university had been shattered by the recent psychological disturbances, I chose to head to the West Coast ski resort with Anthony. So, following the completion of my final exam, we departed, antidepressants in hand, with high hopes that I'd be leaving my troubles behind and embarking on a new life free from pain, chaos, and destruction.

CHAPTER THREE

# Nowhere to Run

*D*ay 5: I have not yet left my father's house, for I am unable to face the community. In addition to reflecting on my past sexual abuse and mental illness, I have reverted to the anorexic behavior of self-starvation, which I also struggled to overcome in the past. I feel ashamed to be seen at my current weight, since I know this town can be cruel about unusual behavior. I wonder why at age twenty-four I still cannot eat "normally" but rather live in a world of all or nothing, either consuming everything I can find or starving myself.

One thing I know is that I revert to past unhealthy behavior when I experience stress—like the stress of coming home. These self-defeating actions then take over and leave me feeling helpless, in a state similar to the paralysis the abuse imprinted on me. Having allowed myself to be pushed into a dark corner by all this internal turmoil, I must now break free of my imprisonment.

The day's submarine sandwich, slid under the door, propels me into the past once again.

When we arrived on the West Coast, Anthony, four of his closest friends, and I, at age nineteen, moved into a large house with two men from Australia. Because I was the only woman, and therefore not having to compete for attention, I felt safe. I applied for my first job—hostess and waitress at a restaurant. Soon I started making friends with my coworkers and having new experiences, but it bothered Anthony to see me growing and changing. One time I went out without him to Hannah's "Sugar Chalet," a

17

coworker's house occupied by four women ranging in age from nineteen to twenty-five. There we played drinking games and then went to a local nightclub to meet some cooks from work. I was having a great time until Anthony showed up and witnessed me dancing with men who, although familiar to me, were strangers to him. In a fit of rage, he bolted onto the dance floor, pushed me down, and called me a slut in front of my coworkers. I was mortified, and everyone stared, wondering why I would allow someone to treat me in such a manner. What they didn't know was that Anthony had just as much trouble as I had coping with my childhood sexual abuse and that while his temper was now indeed driving me away, in the privacy of our home I was the physical and verbal abuser.

One night, after a domestic fight that led to a breakup with Anthony, I arrived at work distraught. Two of my supervisors, Trent and Kelly, noticed that I had been crying and, following our evening work-shift, took me out on the town. After becoming intoxicated at a local bar, Trent, Kelly, one of the cooks, and I went to Trent's house, where Kelly and I became sexually intimate. Trent, who moonlighted as a photographer, took pictures of what was my first lesbian experience. I developed a crush on Kelly, but it was unrequited since she was not actually bisexual.

Next, Trent developed an infatuation with me. And although I was only interested in a friendship, I strung him along for support and connections around town.

Because Anthony did not believe I intended to leave him, I wanted to make him hate me so the breakup would be mutual. A perfect opportunity to provoke his animosity arose when I had the chance to sleep with Peter. The next morning, I confided this to Anthony, sealing our fate.

I ended up moving into the Sugar Chalet and sharing a room with my coworker Kim. I cannot recall a time in my life when I was more confused about sexual orientation. The first night after the other girls had left for the bar, Hannah and I not only shared a bottle of tequila but also our first and last kiss. Between my feelings for Hannah, my crush on Kelly, dates with Trent, and a new sexual attraction I had developed for the prep cook Daren, I didn't know if I was a lesbian, straight, or bisexual. The abuse had skewed all boundaries between heterosexual and homosexual intimacy, to the point where any adult showing me love or able to gratify me in some crazy way was perceived as a potential sexual partner. It didn't matter whether they had tits or testicles.

Trent's manner of buying my affection reminded me a lot of how my father had always acted toward me. At the first sign that I was pulling away, both Trent and my father would do something to make me more dependent on them, invariably diminishing my self-worth. Besides giving me free snowboard equipment, Trent had also introduced me to new drugs— ecstasy and cocaine—which he furnished free when I provided sex. Just as I had allowed my father to buy my silence, I allowed Trent to do the same. As a result of my confusion about these new relationships and my association of sex with love, I became promiscuous and bent on destructive behavior. When Hannah felt enamored of a waiter named Darrel while Kelly was dating him, I decided to investigate this man, eventually seducing him. Hannah never did find out. And while my intention was never to hurt Hannah, subconsciously I resented her for ceasing to take interest in me after we had kissed. In time, my anger toward her proved to be significant and devastating.

At age nineteen I became self-conscious of my body for the first time. I was five feet four inches and weighed 130 pounds, having gained 15 pounds as a result of drinking six nights a week, food bingeing after work, and lack of exercise. My New Year's resolution for 1996 was to get back into shape for the superficial purpose of being a "hottie" in time for a planned trip to Mexico during spring break. Hannah joined me on my quest to lose weight, and we exercised vigorously but still ate and drank in the same fashion, so I didn't lose much weight. From this time on, weight became a constant issue for me, and later I would become obsessive about exercise as a means of weight loss.

Hannah, on the other hand, was losing weight. And during our trip to Mexico, the reason for it became clear—she was bulimic. Having observed her technique of bingeing then mysteriously slipping away to purge in the washroom, I decided to try it myself. I found it painful and repulsive to induce vomiting, eventually deciding that I wanted out of this lifestyle. So when Hannah and the other three original tenants decided to move at the end of the year, Kim and I rented a small one-bedroom apartment. Unfortunately, it was not long before Kim became possessive of our friendship and I felt like I was suffocating.

By September 1996, I had become determined to regain my health and accept new changes and challenges. First, I gave up purging. Then I took a job coaching gymnastics, hoping to set an example of wellness and ensure that girls weren't subjected to the usual weigh-ins and the pressure of dieting at a young age. I started to envy the thin, toned bodies of prepubescent girls, however, so I joined the local gym. Unaware that my addictive personality would eventually have me abusing anything that felt good, and soon started going to the gym seven days a week.

Meanwhile, I realized that since coaching wasn't paying the bills, I needed a night job as well. I was hired at the ski resort's largest nightclub because the boss, Duncan, liked my outgoing personality, although I later found out he liked more than that. I started the nightclub job as a coat-check girl and within two days was promoted to waitress because Duncan appreciated my "work ethic." Most of the other employees were career waitresses who had learned to be deceitful in order to earn big bucks, but one waitress, Gwen—a hustler known as "Diamond Lil"— asked me to move in with her and became very protective of me. Since I was now working five nights a week, I was sure my drinking days were behind me, but as it turned out, alcohol consumption was practically part of the job description.

Soon I accepted a new job Duncan created for me, as a bathtub beer girl, which involved dancing around the tub all night, flirting with clients and making fast cash. I thrived on the sex appeal and power of the position. Even though I now weighed 115 pounds again, I was far from being satisfied with my physical appearance in my skimpy tops and felt I needed to work out more intensely. Typically my day consisted of working out at the gym in the morning, participating in sports while coaching in the afternoon, taking a yoga or kickboxing class at dinnertime, working from 9:00 p.m. to 3:00 a.m., and then drinking from 3:00 a.m. to 5:00 a.m. In time, Gwen introduced me to a world of cocaine and gambling, convincing me to play poker for money. Only after losing a lot of money did I finally step out of denial and see that Gwen was a manipulating coke addict who would do anything to get her fix. Having spent Christmas together high, I knew I would have to get out from under her control, but in the meantime I found other distractions.

With a new job came a new group of men who showered me with attention that ultimately led to empty sex and unrequited love. One man in particular captured my affection—Alex, who was handsome and, although old enough to be my father, had a young soul. He also had all the control and I did as he pleased. I knew Alex was using me, but lacked the self-esteem to think I deserved better. I trusted that if I waited long enough, Alex would realize that with me he could have a partner to love him unconditionally, but fortunately that never occurred.

The time had come to get away from Gwen. Madeline, the head waitress, had inside information on a "house cleaning" that was about to occur, meaning our boss was preparing to fire all those who had been using cocaine on the job. Fortunately, I had never used while working, but had instead relied on alcohol to provide me with the courage I so desperately needed. As a result of the boss's campaign, Gwen was fired the next Saturday night and I was in a new apartment by Sunday morning.

For the first time since age sixteen, I had a place to myself and could live the lifestyle I pleased without anyone judging me. I could eliminate the temptation to eat by keeping the fridge empty of food, I could be obsessive about exercising, and I could invite men over without creating tomorrow's gossip—in short, I had real control. My weight dropped below 100 pounds.

With my new, in-shape body and the attention I was receiving from the male clientele at the nightclub, I started to acquire a false sense of self-esteem. Wanting to have control over men, I used my body to seduce them, taking pleasure in knowing that I had the choice whether to gratify them or not. Never before had I felt power over the male gender. The easiest targets were men in long-term relationships who wanted something new and exciting. And since I never allowed myself to become emotionally attached, I didn't get hurt. But it was a dangerous game to play, because unbeknownst to me I was hurting my self-respect and dignity.

Meanwhile, the power had become an addiction, and I proceeded to seduce my boss. I thought I was special and believed him when he said it was his first time committing adultery. So desperate was I to maintain control over others that I didn't see my own life spinning rapidly out of control as I exercised even more and steadfastly avoided food.

The hatred I felt for myself and my lifestyle had been festering for some time, and being the center of attention was losing its appeal. The final blow to my self-esteem came when I saw Duncan at our staff party with his wife. We had agreed earlier in the day to meet at my place after the party, but suddenly seeing him made me realize that it was I who was being used. To get revenge, I wanted him to see me with another man and feel as jealous and insignificant as I had. So I spent the evening draped over Alex, using the one person for whom I had true feelings.

At the end of the night, Alex and I decided to go back to his place. As we started to become intimate, I felt an urge to confess—I wanted to tell him about Duncan, the awful person I had become, and that I loved him. Instead Alex, who was sexually frustrated and high, became violent, throwing me around the room, calling me a tease and a whore, and saying that women like me were a dime a dozen. His words exactly reflected how I viewed myself, and when he threw me outside bleeding and half-dressed, I reacted pathetically, begging at his door for a second chance. Conditioned to believe from an early age that I was obligated to fulfill men's desires, I felt compelled to clear up my mistake.

The next day, although an emotional wreck with a black eye, I summoned the courage to go to work and talk to Duncan. He was more interested in why I had gone home with Alex than he was in being supportive. I couldn't avoid seeing Alex and being reminded that he viewed me as nothing, or looking at Duncan and knowing he had used me. It was later that I realized my eating disorder reflected my lack of self-esteem and the underlying belief that I was not worthy of food.

I started calling my brother Lance more often, reaching out for his love and support. Lance eventually flew to the West Coast to be with me for a week and, after taking one look at my now 90-pound frame, knew I needed help. Trying to reassure him, I said, "It's not like I look like Kate Moss," to which he replied, "You look worse than Kate Moss . . . Sara, you're anorexic." Only later was I to learn that anorexia nervosa is a psychological illness that causes a person to practice self-starvation as a way of coping with difficult life circumstances. People with anorexia have an intense fear of food and weight, usually developing rigid rules and beliefs about how many calories they can consume in a day, having "forbidden" foods, and eating in a ritualistic manner. Although they deny their hunger, and the fact that they have a problem, people suffering from anorexia usually have an intense preoccupation with eating, even dreaming about it. Such individuals frequently maintain a body weight 15 percent below their average recommended weight, but due to a distorted body image, they often still feel fat. Even though individuals suffering from anorexia have similar symptoms, such as absence of menstrual cycles, they have each developed the illness for different reasons related to their unique psychological and emotional situations.

Soon after his arrival, Lance took me to a doctor, who confirmed the diagnosis and told me to go home and drink Boost, a high-calorie source of essential vitamins and minerals. Lance then found a physician who agreed to see me weekly, at which point I began to eat full meals. I felt so loved by Lance that it was easy for me to eat in his company, but after he returned home I unable to take responsibility for nourishing myself and reverted to old thoughts of worthlessness. After a week of self-starving, going to the gym, and working two jobs, my body was on the verge of failing—although the truth is I was failing my body. Saturday night during last call, one of my usual clients approached me, intoxicated, and said, "Sara, are you anorexic? You are too skinny and you look sick." I burst into tears, ran to the staff room, and collapsed from exhaustion. Alex, who had witnessed the conversation, followed me. At that moment, I didn't care about the past and just wanted Alex to hold me, which he did, although it was to be the last time we saw each other.

After work, my friends took me to the local hospital, where I was given an IV drip for a few hours to treat electrolyte imbalance and severe dehydration, then sent home. By morning I could not get out of bed, and my friends had to literally pick me up and take me to my doctor since my weight had dropped to nearly 85 pounds. She wanted to send me to a city hospital for in-patient care, but when I declined she phoned my mother who, after arriving and barely recognizing me due to my emaciated condition, convinced me to come home temporarily.

## CHAPTER FOUR

# Dying Inside

*D**ay 8:* This cool September day I managed to leave the house for the first time since moving back to my hometown. I was not able to leave my car, however, due to shame about my appearance and lack of progress in life. Instead, I drove around surveying the place, feeling like an outsider haunted by painful reminders of the past.

The leaves, clinging fervently to their boughs as they prepare for an autumn display, make me wonder if I too can be homebound while getting ready for a new future. I occasionally catch myself reflecting on my father's apparent ability to move forward, in contrast with my own agonizing paralysis. How odd that I would allow my adult self to be victimized by my father in this way. I need to remember that things are not destined to continue on as they were before, that I must take responsibility for my very thoughts, that life has many seasons.

As before, the past intrudes on my awareness of the present.

Within three days of my return home with my mother in July 1997, I decided not to go back to the West Coast and my old corrupt lifestyle but to live with self-dignity and moral values. Aware that my illness had served the unexpected purpose of helping me gain my mother's attention, I also wanted to be assured that her love for me was genuine, and not based on pity.

Despite the affection and concern of my mother, sister, and brother, I knew that I alone would have to be responsible for my recovery. In the past, I had sought to regain my health partially for the sake of friends and family; but with anorexia nervosa, things would be different. No one can make an individual with anorexia want to live, because the disorder is a slow emotional and physical suicide, meaning that the desire to live must come from one's own heart and soul. Although other people can serve as stepping stones on the road to recovery, it is up to those suffering from the disorder to do the required work. .

I was now willing to work hard to recover, but I also wanted total control over the process, which made my recovery problematic. I decided that I would gain weight only through muscle mass acquired through working out with a trainer and would eat healthy foods with the assistance of a dietician. My mother took me to our family doctor, however, who immediately advised against my program—counsel I experienced as power used against me once again. Knowing I could not tolerate a treatment plan that robbed me of control, I became determined to find a doctor who would support my recovery program.

My mother then took me to see Dr. Black, who seemed to understand my goals but then said he could hospitalize me, a statement I interpreted as another assertion of power. When I tried to leave, he locked the door, and in a state of panic I threw a tantrum, yelling to my mother in the hallway. By the time he allowed for my escape, he had convincingly demonstrated how strongly I needed to be in control of my life. In retrospect, I know we cannot control the hand we are dealt, but we can control how we choose to play the cards.

After seeing many different dieticians and doctors, I finally found a pair that suited me. Still intent on maintaining control, however, I began lying, manipulating, and refusing to cooperate with their team efforts. Eventually I stopped working with the dietician, as she was costly and unable to inspire my participation. But I did continue to see the doctor, who supported my personal goals, including workouts at the gym.

The gym I joined had certain regulations—among them, I had to work with a personal trainer and have physical checkups to confirm that working out was not hazardous to my health. Gretchen, my trainer, went well beyond the call of duty. Upon learning of my illness, she researched it; when I wanted to give up, she motivated me to keep fighting; when my weight dropped to a point where I could no longer work out, she invited my family and friends to her home for support meetings.

While on the West Coast, I had burned bridges with many of my former friends, but not Anna or her roommate Tammy. And by July 1997 I had become dependent on their support, even though they did not understand anorexia. For example, I could not eat while alone, so at night they would meet me at their apartment for supper. On such occasions, they witnessed my obsession with food. I had to cook our meals to ensure that I had total control over the foods I was consuming. Not only that, but I had to weigh each portion in order to determine exactly how many calories would be entering my body—information I was able to access by using my two food scales, three body scales, and approximately twenty books on nutrition and calorie counting. Moreover, I was extremely phobic about certain ingredients I considered "toxic," so everything had to be natural, as well. I also kept a lengthy list of refreshments I regarded as "forbidden," such as junk food. Throughout, I relied heavily Anna and Tammy for reassurance, especially when I felt fat at 85 pounds.

Perhaps the most important aspect of our friendship was Anna and Tammy's ability to laugh with me when I joked about anorexia, whereas other people were offended by these shenanigans. One night while Anna and I were in a restaurant, the people across from us were staring and whispering about how thin I was. So when I got up to use the washroom, I deliberately collapsed over their table, told them I was starving, and asked if I could have their rolls. They regarded me with astonishment as I proudly walked back to my table with all their rolls.

Eventually realizing that my illness was too big a responsibility for my family and friends, I decided to seek professional help from someone who understood it. The only such specialist in my hometown, Kayla, was too busy to accept new clients but referred me to a nursing student, who proved to be supportive and nonjudgmental. I, in turn, provided her with insight into the world of an anorexic.

Finding extra time on my hands, I accepted a part-time position as a waitress at a small tearoom managed by Tammy. Although the job didn't pay well, the staff championed my efforts to overcome my illness. Some of the patrons, on the other hand, did not. One night while serving tea and pie to older women, I overheard one of them saying I reminded her of a model named Twiggy. How she could find me beautiful when it was clear I was suffering from a devastating disease was beyond my comprehension. It was then that I realized my illness had nothing to do with wanting to be attractive but was instead an outward expression of the pain I felt internally, an obvious cry for help.

At work and elsewhere, many people offered advice, some sharing information about their own eating disorders and others delivering what they claimed were spiritual messages from a higher power. Not being spiritual at the time, I found the latter incidents bizarre, but they happened so frequently I eventually could no longer write them off as coincidences. For example, once I was in a bulk-food store when an old woman seemed to appear out of nowhere; placing her hands on me, she declared that God understood the pain I was in, that I had more challenges ahead, and not to be scared because I would get through them, then quickly disappeared. Now I better understand the idea that a person receptive to seeing shall receive the gift of sight, but in the fall of 1997 I needed a loud message to jump-start my faith.

Throughout this time, I made an effort to break free of my destructive habits. I ceased drinking—not because of health concerns but out of my commitment to reduce caloric intakes and my resentment at feeling out of control while under the influence. I also stopped using hard drugs, because I was no longer familiar with the dealers in my hometown, and marijuana because of the feeling of hunger it brought on. I went from being aggressive to passive, since I didn't have the mental, emotional, or physical strength to engage in violence. I was no longer promiscuous, for I had lost my sex drive, and perhaps my sex appeal, due to malnourishment. I even started a gratitude journal, giving thanks for the willpower to not eat, the energy that coffee supplied, the appetite-suppressing cigarettes I smoked, every pound I had lost, and for not getting caught when I manipulated my weight. Later I discovered that until your intentions are aligned with your well-being, you cannot transform yourself.

Soon the tearoom shut down and I was hired at a pub where my sister, Jackie, worked. This was an opportunity to spend time with Jackie and once again surround myself with love and support. But in my spare time I was still consumed with my depressing situation and deep feelings of hopelessness. I wanted to keep my life in constant motion to avoid contemplating food, but I didn't take into account the obvious—that you can't run from your thoughts.

One day after a busy lunch hour at the pub, I encountered a woman named Daffony, whom I had trained with in gymnastics and who was now head coach for a women's competitive team. When I told her about my coaching experience, she encouraged me to speak with her employer, Jenna, about a possible job at her sports club. En route to the interview I was extremely nervous, not knowing what Jenna would think about my illness and wanting to make it clear that I would never impose my eating problems on students. I also prayed that she shared my beliefs about training: fun first, no forced weigh-ins or diets, and freedom from competition. Fortunately both Jenna and the other club members had compassion toward my illness, as did the athletes and their parents.

While struggling with my illness, I considered religion as a means of support. Anna, whose father was a minister, suggested we attend church to pray. It had been thirteen years since I had been in a church, and though we followed his advice I didn't know how to pray for the strength and courage I so desperately needed. While the church setting provided some comfort, in the end we both knew I needed to find a treatment facility as time was running out.

The closest treatment option was as an outpatient in the city where my brother lived, sixteen hours from my hometown. As it turned out, Anna wanted to attend a school there, and since I had become dependent on her, sharing an apartment seemed like a perfect solution. Because I was too weak to travel, Anna and my father made the sixteen-hour trip each weekend to look for an apartment. But no sooner had they found one than Anna notified me that she would be making the move alone. I felt too rejected to ask why. Later I learned it was because of the severity of my illness: Anna was sure I was dying and did not want my deteriorating state to weigh on her conscience.

With no ready access to a treatment facility, it became essential to strike a balance between independence and support from the people around me. Although Tammy was hurt that Anna had abruptly moved out, she held no hostile feelings toward me but instead took care of me. She warmed up my car's engine during the winter and wrapped me in blankets when I was chilled. She looked out for my well-being at social functions too, and when I was offered the sports bar job on weekends, she worked several night shifts for me. Also, when I was unable to get out of bed, or confused due to malnourishment that affected my brain, she would reassure me. Sources of support at the sports bar included Gretchen's bartender husband; my old friend Kathy, a waitress; and even my boss, who had given me a job selling cheap shooters and cans of beer, and allowed me flexibility due to my illness.

Still, my physical condition declined, until I eventually weighed about 70 pounds. By then, my hair was falling out; my teeth were cracking; my legs were often blue due to lack of circulation; I had grown soft, fine hair called lanugo all over my body and face, which kept me warm; and people had to help me up stairs, a challenge the wasted muscle tissue in my legs could not undertake on its own. Lab work revealed that I was in the early stages of osteoporosis. I couldn't sleep. I often wet the bed because my pelvic-floor muscles had deteriorated. In response to the malnourishment, my mental functioning had greatly diminished. I was dangling tenuously from a rapidly unwinding thread called life. The only benefit to having me as an employee was that I excelled at selling drinks to the public, who pitied my condition.

In addition to my physical condition, my home life too had eroded. I had moved in with my mother and begun making her life miserable, cranking up the thermostat to the highest possible setting just to stay warm, throwing out her newly purchased groceries, and plagued by spells of forgetfulness, introducing an endless stream of precarious situations. For example, once after locking myself out of the house, I scaled a side wall and climbed in an open bathroom window, landing in a handstand on the toilet, which caused my arms to give out. Another time I locked myself out after warming up my car in my pajamas on a bitterly cold winter day, and since I didn't have the strength to kick in my mother's front door, I convinced a neighbor's roofer to do it, but in the process he splintered the door frame. This incident forced my mother out of her own home, for she could no longer tolerate living with me. She moved in with her best friend Janice and began checking on me each morning to make sure I was breathing in my sleep. I can only imagine the horror she must have felt upon entering her home not knowing if her daughter would be dead or alive.

Improper brain functioning caused me other difficulties as well. Daily, I would forget my name and where I was or what I was doing, and I needed others to remind me. After such incidents, whoever was with me would say something like, "Sara, the lights were on but no one was home." If I was alone, I would attempt to orient myself by performing a familiar task. One evening, my brain malfunctioned as I was buying my customary black coffee at a drive-through window, and all I could do was cruise through again and again, with the employees looking at me as if I were crazy. Most often I would attempt to get back on track by going to a local grocery store and staring at food labels.

At the time, I weighed about 65 pounds and had managed to avoid hospitalization because I, like all anorexics, was a master of manipulation. I had refused to take my mother, sister, and brother's advice to see a psychiatrist, because I was in denial about anorexia nervosa being a mental illness, believing it was instead a physically debilitating outcome of starvation. I had no idea that the starvation originates in an underlying psychological disturbance.

My doctor, meanwhile, had moved out of town and I had started seeing a new physician named Dr. Maguire. While at her office, I could not hide my low blood pressure or skeletal face, but did cheat about my weight, taping rolls of coins around my waist then persuading the secretary to weigh me with my track suit on by claiming I was too cold to undress. I was learning how anorexics manipulate weight to serve their illness. My next learning opportunity came soon after, when Dr. Maguire, having agreed not to hospitalize me as long as I kept my weight above 85 pounds, asked me to consider voluntary admission at a local psychiatric hospital. I consented to go in February—after Christmas and my sister's January wedding—although I never intended to follow through, confident that death was close at hand.

Christmas of 1997 was a time of great significance for me, because I was now sure this would be my last holiday season with my family. It became essential to personalize my gifts so they would reflect the love and gratitude I felt toward each family member, including my father. But at the same time, I didn't want to dampen their spirits with gifts that said good-bye.

My thoughts during my sister's wedding were even more morbid. Because I was the maid of honor, Jackie had made special arrangements for me—a seat at the front of the church in case I got tired, a salad prede-livered to the reception, and a dress designed with a fleece liner to hide my cadaverous frame. And yet, I experienced the ceremony as a premonition of my own funeral proceedings: being in a church with everyone I loved, beautiful music playing, a minister saying a prayer to God, and a reception afterward. It made me sad to think that at my memorial service I would be unable to overtly express my love.

Despite these aberrant thoughts, I made it through the wedding just fine, except that I almost forgot my name when it came time to sign the marriage license. Then at the reception I lost control, drinking too much because I felt it would be my last gathering with family and friends. Now sadness surfaced only when I approached my grandfather for one of his famous bear hugs and he hardly recognized me because of my fragile con-dition. Otherwise, I delighted in telling people, as I later learned, either "Good-bye, I'm going home to die," or its opposite, "I was going to kill myself tonight, but now I realize that I want to live!"

By the time I arrived at my mother's house, intoxication had drained me of willpower, and I could not resist eating "forbidden foods" left over from the rehearsal dinner the night before. I knew if I started I would not stop, and I intended to wash the food down with sleeping pills so this would literally be my "last supper." After three hours of indulging, I lit a candle that Lance had given me years before and wrote my mother, Jack-ie, and Lance a brief letter of apology. Upon finishing, I swore I would never be able to forgive myself if I were to live past sunrise.

The next morning as the sun arced through the sky, my mother returned to find me on the family room couch surrounded by empty pill bottles. Though she looked confused, she did not call for help, probably because she concluded I was well and she viewed the incident as yet another of my pleas for attention. Determined to avert discussion, I snatched the letter from the pillow beside me and headed straight for my bedroom.

When I awoke again that night, I was hallucinating and experienced diminished motor skills, along with the distinct sensation that I was going to die. Then suddenly I realized that I did not want to die now, not like this. In sheer panic and desperation, I reached for the phone. Too frightened to dial 911, I called my mother and Lance, but no one was home at either house. And although I tried to leave a message on Janice's answering machine, my words came out slurred.

Someone must have been watching out for me that night. Lance, dining at a restaurant with my father, had dashed off sensing I was in serious trouble, blazed through a bad storm with an engine that stalled intermittently, and somehow arrived in time to convince me to go to the hospital. I can only imagine the picture I must have presented as I ran through the emergency room doors screaming, a skeleton in motion with crazy bed-head hair, wearing hot pink fleece pants plus my mother's oversized boots, and yelling in slurred speech, "I took some pills. If I'm only tripping out, then I'm going to leave; but if I'm about to die, then I'll stay." Teetering on a precipice where life meets death, I wanted desperately to be saved.

Then, I had the most spiritual experience of my life. I left my body and entered the divine light, experiencing a feeling of utter peace. I no longer feared death but knew that if I should die, it would only be the end of my physical body while my soul would live on. As much as I wanted to stay in this blissful state, something told me I still had much to do on earth, but I seemed to lack the strength necessary to leave the light and reenter my cold, weak body. At that moment I heard a voice like my mother's, saying, "You can't die. All you have to do is get up and say you're a fighter." I glanced down from where I seemed to be floating and noticed Lance telling me, "Look into my eyes." When I opened my eyes I saw, staring back at me, an angel whose energy passed through me, infusing my body with strength enough for me to declare, "I'm a fighter."

# CHAPTER FIVE

# A Second Chance

*D*ay *12:* Often my father brings up the past to make sense of it and to apologize for his actions. At such times he talks about being very ill and depressed during the 1980s and says he has recently been diagnosed with a dissociative disorder that, according to his psychiatrist, prevents him from retrieving full recollections of the abuse. He explains that he cannot bear to think of the monster he once was; hearing this, a part of me seizes up inside thinking that his blood courses through me, that my illness may be in some way affiliated with his genes. I also feel an odd sense of empathy, however, and although I will never understand why anyone would sexually abuse their own child, I do recognize the intense impact a mental illness can have on one's thoughts and behaviors.

Today I told my father that although we can't change the past we also never have to relive it. Now that we have confronted each other concerning the sexual abuse and verified previously blocked memories, we both need to stop dwelling on possible causes for the abuse, because in the process of trying to find an answer each of us loses a piece of our sanity. Instead, I tell my father, individually we have a rare opportunity to start over and that we each need to seek our own personal remedy in order to heal. The fact that I have chosen to stop running and face the source of my terror will hopefully free me from the pain associated with it.

The first time I stopped running was by circumstance, as I recall, not choice.

After I was taken to the hospital and put in Cardiac Care in January 1998, my mother and Janice spent the night sleeping in chairs by my side. When I saw daylight streaming in through the curtains and knew I had survived, I felt euphoric. I tried to explain to my mother what I had experienced—being out of my body, the light, her voice, Lance, the angel, and my realization that it wasn't my time to go. I told her I now had faith in a higher being, and that I believed I had a purpose as part of a master plan here on earth. I concluded that even if this series of events was merely a hallucination prompted by the overdose, it was nevertheless a profound spiritual experience. Immediately the old woman I had met nearly six months before in the bulk-food store entered my room and, probably recalling our brief encounter, sat on the edge of my bed. Her husband had just passed away after a lengthy battle with cancer, she explained, and she wanted me to know for sure that God was with me, an occurrence that confirmed in my mind that I had indeed been in a spiritual realm.

The next day, the cardiologist greeted me by calling me Alice. He added, by way of explanation, that a drug contained in the pills I had taken can cause a person to act crazy, so he called it the "Mad Hatter drug."

I had my mother bring in my books on nutrition so I would be prepared if the staff tried forcing me to eat "forbidden foods." Then I had a visit from Terry, a childhood friend whose mother was dying of cancer but wanted to live, and the contrast between her inability to live and my attempt at killing myself shocked me into admitting that anorexia was psychological and required treatment in the psychiatric ward. I also received the gift of a journal, which soon inspired me to begin writing about my experiences in order to heal, faithfully dating each entry as I set pen to paper.

At first, upon opening my journal I would start talking to God, seeking answers to questions concerning my life and purpose. Above all, I wanted to know if he would forgive me for attempting suicide, which I had learned was considered a sin in his eyes. Then on February 3, while in search of higher truths about life and death as I strolled past the elevators outside the cardiac care unit, I nearly collided with a woman named Kate, whose daughter, Mandy, had been my friend at age ten. At the time, my family was so dysfunctional I would escape to sip tea with Kate, even when

Mandy wasn't home, because I emulated this woman's projection of family life. Unfortunately, fate was cruel to her: her son was killed in a drunk driving accident when he was nineteen, and years later her husband left her. Kate, who had never so much as attended church, subsequently became a chaplain. While reflecting on Kate's life, I learned that bad things can happen to good people—a discovery that shed light on the fact that the sexual abuse I suffered as a child, and the anorexia I was currently dealing with, did not mean I was a bad person.

On that February day, Kate asked me to reminisce about the happier times in her life, when her son and her marriage were alive, I think she wanted to show me that once a person knows happiness they can always find it again. I, on the other hand, needed her to confirm that as a child I'd had many good qualities; that the sexual abuse I suffered then, as well as the anorexia I was currently dealing with, did not mean I was a bad person; and that I, like her, carried a palpable potential for happiness in the future. This she did, adding the message that God loves me unconditionally and is forgiving. Then, after reciting a prayer, she looked at me and said, "I can see that one day you are going to blossom into a beautiful sunflower." That image seeded in my mind a symbol of how I wanted my life to feel once I was healed.

Shortly after sunset I was informed that the next morning I would be transferred to the psychiatric ward, which proved to be both worse and better than I had imagined. It was moments after arriving that I began journaling intensively, to retain whatever sanity I could.

*February 4, 1998:* Three people escorted me to this ward, making me feel like a common criminal. Then they went through my personal belongings, an invasion of my privacy, and took away all objects considered dangerous. I had to speak up on my own behalf, so I asked for the return of my nail clippers and said that if I wasn't back in ten minutes, to send in the troops—a comment they didn't find the least bit funny.

I haven't seen anyone in a straight jacket, but I did hear eerie screams coming from the "rubber rooms" behind the nurses' station. The patients are scary, silent and just staring. Lights out is at 11:00 p.m., hard with my insomnia, and you are not allowed to leave your room until 7:00 a.m. I can't go off the ward, but there is a smoking patio, one TV, and pay phones. Until my program is set up, I have to eat what is sent to me and then sit at the table for an hour afterward, reflecting on what I have just eaten.

On the upside, I have a private room with a bathroom containing a toilet and sink, a bath, a desk, chairs for visitors, and permission for my mother to bring in my CD player. I am confused about why they lock my bathroom door, but maybe they assume I am bulimic. As I gain weight, I won't have to worry about pressures from a society constantly emphasizing weight loss and body image. The best part of my first day here was connecting to the night nurse Linda, who kindly stayed and talked with me for an hour after my meal. Maybe this place isn't going to be bad, although I haven't exactly started singing the famous song from *Annie*, "I think I'm going to like it here . . ." No matter what happens, I am confident these people will never break my spirit.

*February 5:* Today I feel a little more settled in my new environment. I met a nurse named Tina, who is about my age and engaged to Jeffery, a man I knew in high school. She radiated positive energy, keeping my spirits up. I also met a few patients who apologized for not greeting me yesterday, explaining that they had been terrified by my appearance since I looked like "walking death." My already distorted body image has been further challenged by the fact that yesterday I was wearing red plaid flannel pajama bottoms, and today a three-hundred-pound man is wearing similar pajamas, insisting they are mine.

*February 6:* I haven't seen Dr. Black yet, apparently because he considers my brain too malnourished to help me converse, although to me I seem acutely aware of my present circumstances. I have met Eve, my dietician, and we appear to be headed for a love-hate relationship since she is making me give up many of my nutritional practices—including vegetarianism, eating only natural foods, having nothing but fruit until noon, and avoiding dairy—despite the fact that I am lactose intolerant.

She might succeed in changing my eating habits for a few months, but she can't make the decisions for me once I leave. I do hope she will teach me how to eat in a normal manner. I am scared that I may end up becoming a compulsive binge eater, but she assures me that this will never happen. Right now I feel as though my life is all about eating; yet living to eat makes no sense compared with eating in order to live.

*February 8:* My anorexic side is conniving, causing me to lose 3 pounds since I have been here, while my rational side is wondering what the staff is going to do to me. One thing I know for certain is that they expect me to gain 2.2 pounds per week.

*February 9:* Tomorrow is my first case conference, when my psychiatrist, psychologist, social worker, dietician, occupational therapist, and nurse get together to discuss my treatment program. Linda advised me to write a letter stating my treatment goals. Although I did this, none of my goals were included in the contract that was prepared. Moreover, I was not allowed to attend the conference, so I waited in my bedroom with butterflies in my stomach, until I was notified that my program is to be based on punishment versus privilege: if I gain weight, I will be rewarded; if I lose weight, I forfeit a privilege. In addition, I am on "bedroom arrest" and permitted to leave for only thirty minutes during mealtimes plus three smoking breaks per day; I am to rest on my bed for an hour after each meal; and my bathroom is to be locked at all times. Thus, my life has come under the total control of others—circumstances I instinctively rebel against, as well as anything else associated with my history of childhood sexual abuse.

When I cried and asked a staff member, Tina, why I had received such harsh treatment, she replied, "It's going to be a long and rocky road," but expressed confidence that I can overcome my illness if I follow the program and have the desire to heal.

*February 10:* This day was not pleasant. For one thing, it seems wrong to make me, an antisocial anorexic with a fear of food, become more introverted by requiring me to stay in my room with my life revolving around mealtimes. Angry that they were controlling my body by forcing me to eat, I started calculating what it would take to gain enough weight to get out of the hospital. Next I figured out how many peanut butter sandwiches I would have to eat given that 1 pound equaled 3,500 calories and each slice of bread had 60 calories; each portion of peanut butter had 98; and each pat of margarine 100. Then in a rage and on a mission, I stormed out to the kitchen, where I made enough sandwiches to gain a pound, yelling at the nurses, "You want me to gain weight, well here's the first pound!" I took the sandwiches to my room and started bingeing. A nurse named Diane came to my room and tried to stop me. Acting as if she was a police officer and I a fugitive holding a deadly weapon in my hand, she demanded, "Drop the sandwiches. Step away from them. You're going to get hurt." The warning pertained to the discomfort I would feel if I ate them all. Out of spite, however, I finished the food and ultimately experienced the pain Diane had warned me of.

I was also angry about having my bathroom locked. Each time I needed to use the facilities, I had to ask a nurse to take me, and as a very private individual I felt that having someone watch me urinate was a terrible invasion of my privacy and diminished my dignity. Further, toward the end of the day I felt an urge to have a bowel movement—my first since entering the hospital. When it initially came on, I yelled to the nurses, sarcastically, "Grab some cards. We can have a game of gin, because Sara needs to take a shit."

After hearing about my day, Linda, on the night shift, came to speak with me. I told her how terrified I was that the day might be a sign of things to come, to which she replied, "Instead of worrying about what might happen, take it one day at a time, and remember there may be rough days, but there will be sunny ones, too." She then tucked me in bed with a warm blanket, helping me see that at least I had survived.

*February 16:* Tomorrow is the day for my second case conference. This time they are allowing me to attend, so I would like to present my case, especially the anguish I have been going through during this past week. Being on "bedroom arrest" has definitely taken its toll on me: (1) Confinement has caused me to feel overwhelmed with anxiety, because I am claustrophobic. (2) Breaks and meals have caused me to become compulsive and obsessed with counting time. (3) I'm lonely due to the fact that no patients are permitted to see me. (4) Having no distractions, my mind races with conflicting thoughts. (5) I am constantly on an emotional rollercoaster, mostly depressed. (6) Out of boredom, I spend hours cleaning and pacing. (7) Due to my restricted smoking, I am having withdrawal symptoms in addition to reactions to the treatment for anorexia, but did not come here for tobacco addiction.

*February 17:* When I went to my case conference, things took an unexpected turn, as I was startled by the many people working to help me recover. I felt protected and even loved since these strangers seemed to want me to live, and I realized that the restrictive program they arranged for me had been born out of "tough love." Only a week ago I was angry at them, but now they are the people I most trust—my saviors—and I do not want to let them down. During the conference, my program was not changed, but it hardly seems so bad now that I know their intentions are noble.

*February 23:* Tomorrow is my third case conference. This time I want to show them that I can think clearly so Dr. Black will come talk with me. I want to imprint my thoughts about resenting treatment on the man in charge, if only to feel a sense of connection with him, be reassured of his confidence in my recovery, and know that we will be partners in it.

During the past week, I have tried to analyze what is really going on, which required reassessing my own responsibility for my circumstances. The result was the following: (1) Feeling overwhelmed and anxious comes from losing control and wanting it back, while claustrophobia envelops me when I'm imprisoned by my own thoughts. (2) I do not count time because of my program, I count because of my OCD, and if I wasn't counting time I would be counting calories. (3) I am lonely not because of the confinement but because I am antisocial; in the outside world, I routinely isolated myself in my mother's house. (4) The conflicts I am experiencing occur wherever I go, and reflect my emotional self battling with my rational self. (5) My roller-coaster of emotions is more a physical issue, caused by chemical imbalances rooted in malnutrition. (6) I clean for hours to take out my aggression, and pace to burn calories. (7) I was depressed before I came here, as it was only a month ago that I tried to take my own life. (8) I am getting treatment for anorexia, and restricted smoking is just a small price to pay for improving my health.

*February 24:* On this one-month anniversary since my hospitalization, I attended the case conference, which did not go well. My caregivers were not impressed with my attempts to understand my true feelings, nor did they adequately acknowledge my effort to follow the program. My increase in privileges amounted to two extra fifteen-minute breaks from my room, and only because I now have two more meals—or "snacks," as they call them. This feels more like a punishment, and I am angry again about my lack of control over the program. To regain some control, I intend to manipulate my calorie intake.

This I did by first recording the calories I was consuming. After some calculation, I realized that because my meals were no longer supervised the easiest way to manipulate 400 to 500 calories was to eliminate condiment packages, such as those of peanut butter and margarine, by switching the full ones for the empty ones and later clearing the full packages from my room.

Next, I made up the following exercise program: *Day 1,* work on glutes, quads, hamstrings, thighs, calves, and shins; *Day 2,* work on chest, shoulders, biceps, and triceps; *Every day,* work on abs and do yoga. I timed my exercising perfectly so I would not get caught. Using shampoo bottles taped together for weights, I exercised my chest, arms, and abs on my bed with a blanket over me, so that if a nurse suddenly walked into my room it would look like I was simply taking a nap. Similarly, I performed my leg-toning exercises near my CD player so that anyone who saw me would think I was just changing a CD. I did wall push-ups on a poster that my mother had brought in, so if someone observed me it would appear as if I were straightening the picture; and I worked my biceps and triceps at my desk chair as if quietly reading. Because yoga was more challenging to disguise due to its unusual positions, I would set my alarm clock so I could do my routine after the 5:00 a.m. night check and before the 6:00 a.m. day check. But one morning an attendant checked on me at 5:30 and found me in a pose halfway kissing my ass. When I told him I was meditating, he was as embarrassed as I was and said, "No need to explain."

The manipulation of calories became an addictive game, the object of which was to see how much food I could dispose of without getting caught. Eventually, I was eating only one-fourth of the food that had been delivered to my room. And while my original plan was to control my intake of food, I could see that instead food was once again controlling me. I needed to confide in someone, though I knew that being honest with the staff was tantamount to losing privileges. Finally, I gave Linda my calorie-counting books, knowing she would view this act as a positive step toward recovery.

It was clear that to regain my health I needed a new approach. Not only was my body deteriorating, but my soul too was starting to suffer. So to keep my spirits high, I decided to comply with the program. In addition, I taped personal affirmations around my room for inspiration; had my mother buy me books about spirituality; and stretched out on my bed with her so we could read them together whenever she visited. The power of sharing positive energy changed my perspective on life. It soon became abundantly clear that the other patients were equally in need of positive reinforcement, so each morning during breakfast I read a phrase or a brief passage from one of my books. At first the patients found this practice strange, but as time went on they looked forward to hearing the day's selection. My favorites included "Make peace with imperfection," "Be aware of the snowball effect of your thinking," and "Let go of the idea that gentle, relaxed people can't be superachievers," all adapted from the book *Don't Sweat the Small Stuff ... and it's all small stuff* by Richard Carlson. Most readings segued into morning discussions about ways to apply the day's message to our lives.

Because I enjoyed uplifting the patients, I failed to recognize that it is the staff's obligation, and not mine, to keep up morale. Nor did I consider that working on a psychiatric ward with depressed people can cause staff negativity to spread like wildfire, increasing the difficulty of patient recovery. Later, I registered an awareness of both these realities, and also of the importance of surrounding ourselves with positive influences, filtering out negative energy, and reducing the time spent with "toxic" friends or family members who drain our energy and kill our spirit.

Next, to recapture my sense of humor I became the "class clown," entertaining others. If I spotted extra trays on the meal cart and heard the nurse ask, "Who wants seconds?" I would yell, "I do, I do." When the student nurses put on a game of Bingo and someone won a chocolate bar, I would shout, "Rats, that's what I wanted." Not everyone, however, was well enough to appreciate my jokes. One man, feeling shamed by my comment, went so far as to return his prize. Even though I sometimes laughed so hard I wet my pants, whereupon a physiotherapist would design an exercise drill to help strengthen my pelvic floor muscles, I wholeheartedly welcomed the return of my sense of humor.

All along, one of the most traumatic events of each week was being weighed. Every Tuesday the night shift nurse would wake me early, make me use the toilet, and then weigh me facing the numbers, encouraging me to take responsibility for each pound I had gained or lost. Such moments always aroused ambivalent emotions within me: If I had gained weight, I would at first be reduced to tears, since I viewed gains as giving up a part of myself I had been holding on to and hiding behind, then I would feel joy knowing that weight gain meant an increase of privileges and more approval. By contrast, if I had lost weight, initially the anorexic in me would be delighted, then I would feel down for having forsaken the respect of the staff. Obviously, I needed to examine why I so often clung to my illness and what the payoff was for me.

As the day unfolded, I began to reflect more on my past and focus on aspects necessary for my healing. For example, while wondering why my mother did not protect me from my father's cruel abuses, I realized it was because she didn't know they were occurring. Since my mother grew up in a wholesome household, she would never have considered a father capable of molesting his daughter. Further, even if she had she was too compromised herself to be able to do much of anything; so deep was her depression at the time that it was impossible for her to love anyone, including her daughter or herself. In fact, one day she told me she didn't love me. And while I forgave her, I still could not completely let go of the memory.

Also on this one-month anniversary of my hospitalization, my insatiable need for love began to make sense to me. Once you determine that your own mother doesn't love you, you can't help feeling unwanted and desperately in need of love. At times in my childhood I would fake illness so my mother would stay home from work to care for me, making me tea and toast, combing my hair into pigtails, and cradling me in her arms, saying, "I love you, pumpkin."

Another aspect of myself that I see has been holding me back is my obsession with control. Self-starvation has been a delusional way for me to feel like I have control over my body, but now it is being taken away. Also, male doctors and staff have been triggering the release of long-buried control issues. For example, when Dr. Black takes charge it's as if I'm being violated all over again; and when the night checks are conducted by men, I am reminded of my father's entries into my room as I lay sleeping.

For defensive purposes, the mind often acts like an overheated hair dryer, shutting down until it has cooled off enough to once again process stored information. Unfortunately we cannot choose what to remember but must wait for the mind to retrieve hidden information on its own. There are many ways memory can come back—in flashbacks, dreams, and events that trigger sensory data—and this tends to happen serendipitously, for no apparent reason. This process of becoming conscious of memories is often frustrating because it occurs piecemeal over time. But at least now I can see a bigger picture of forces guiding my behavior: in order to cope with memory fragments of abuse, I had shifted my focus to food and weight.

Along with feelings of frustration at fragmentary memory retrieval, I am enraged because my father has started to visit me. *Why am I in a psychiatric ward,* I wonder, *when he is sicker than I ever was?* At times I feel such intense anger that I want to be violent and aggressive again, to break everything in sight and put my fist through walls. Instead, I suppress my rage, which also is not a healthy way to work through issues.

My personal view on parenting is that having healthy sperm or fertile eggs does not make you a mother or father. An unfit parent is one who cannot provide a child with the necessities of life, including food, shelter, love, positive modeling, a nurturing environment, rules and consequences, and the structure necessary to grow to be a healthy adult. If a person cannot provide such necessities, they should not be a parent. In my case, although I suffered sexual abuse, due to the crisis I have caused, my family life has improved. Sometimes it takes a crisis to pull a family together so that members finally develop strong bonds. While I was the only one in my family to be hospitalized, my anorexia has affected the others, forcing them to face the skeletons in their own closets.

From the beginning of my hospitalization, I had many visitors, including members of the community who came to offer support. People were so generous and compassionate that I was overwhelmed, making it hard to express in words how grateful I was. Visitors were subsequently restricted to "family only," due to a bad flu circulating through the community; and when the ban was lifted, my friends did not return to visit. I felt so rejected, I put a *personal* ban on visitors, deciding to reject rather than be rejected. Perhaps I really was afraid of the outside world.

As time went on, I developed a support network with members of the staff, who approached their caretaking quite individually. Some quickly asserted control, while others judged me and used tough love. A few taught me that, although my behavior was unacceptable, I was still a good person with limitless potential.

Being hospitalized has already taught me many things, especially the fact that I need to take responsibility for my behavior. It is hard to explain why someone manipulates out of self-preservation or acts on distorted beliefs when ill. But ultimately, despite illness, it is necessary to understand the reasons for self-destructive behavior in order to heal.

*February 25:* I am very fortunate to be surrounded by many helpful and friendly caregivers. Most of them make little pay and rarely receive the recognition they so richly deserve. It's a shame, because they are the warriors of this domain, and as such they save lives. Besides Tina and Linda, I favor six nurses, my psychologist, and my occupational therapist above all others, for making a difference in my life:

Leah—Before Leah was assigned to be my nurse, she would frequently visit me just because she wanted to. She seems to understand my illness and is never judgmental. When I am down, she always has a gift to lift my spirits, my favorite being a plaque with an angel on it, and the words "You're not alone." She once told me, "Sara, I like being your nurse, but I love being your friend."

Amy—Despite the fact that Amy is reserved, she is a great listener and shows empathy any time she hears about my problems.

Patricia—Patricia is great at letting me know when I am acting inappropriately. Although her stern nature scares me at times, I see a more comforting individual hiding beneath her gruff exterior.

Diane—Diane always makes me feel human, and we share a love of sunflowers. To me, sunflowers have become symbolic of hope for a better future when I can fulfill my potential. Diane reminds me that I have a bigger role in this world than being just another "psych patient" or "suicide statistic."

Jody—Jody has a bubbly personality that always makes me laugh. Her love for candy continually reminds me that not every woman is obsessed with dieting.

Cara—There are two Caras. One is nurturing and concerned about my well-being, while the other gives me a kick of motivation when I need it and provides inspirational advice, constantly reminding me that it is my choice whether to live as a victim or a survivor.

Melissa—Although she was never assigned to be my nurse and so cannot be counted as one, Melissa has become like a mother. She is one of the most supportive people in my life.

Daniel—Daniel is the psychologist who helps me with my emotional and mental distress. He has provided me with information on anorexia nervosa, OCD, and PTSD, and shown me connections between my symptoms and my past, as well as the steps necessary to overcome my current depression. I know it is up to me to do the work, and he has done a great job of encouraging me. Our first few sessions were a waste, however, as I usually spent the hour sobbing uncontrollably about too much mayo on my tuna sandwich at lunch. But in our first productive session, we talked about the disturbing flashbacks I was experiencing—the vivid mental imagery of my father entering my room at night and the sensory memories of feeling controlled and forced into action against my will—all of which he said marked the initial stages of my healing, for I was recovering my memory. Then this afternoon I happily told Daniel my latest discovery, that the program would in fact work because I could certainly keep gaining weight for privileges, then with the weight on I would be mentally recovered and no longer interested in self-starvation. Daniel always reminds me that it is okay to have negative thoughts and feelings while trying to focus on positive ones.

Karla—Karla, my occupational therapist, has made one of the greatest contributions to my recovery. The more we work together, the more fulfilled I feel emotionally and spiritually. The first assignments she gave me involved expressing myself beyond words, which helped me sense the freeing power of creativity for the first time. As a result, I wrote, drew, painted, sculpted, sewed, and cut, experimenting with many ways to depict inner feelings.

Physically, though, I am in bad shape. I have problems with menstruation, digestion, and elimination. I am anemic, dealing with a vitamin and mineral deficiency. To help correct these problems, I was given Prodium, Colace, calcium, vitamin D, folic acid, B-12, a multivitamin, Prepulsid, and Oval. I also started taking an antidepressant and a sleeping pill at night. In addition, since my immune system was weak and I had exhibited promiscuous behavior in the past, I underwent an HIV test. Waiting for the results seemed eternal, then when they came back negative I believed I had been given a second chance and vowed to save myself for the partner with whom I could spend my life.

Soon after this reprieve, a humiliating experience at mealtime revealed that I was a wreck not only physically but also mentally. I had eaten a half grapefruit the way I always did, cutting the pieces into triangles and scooping them out with my spoon. But the nurse on duty, insisting that I had intentionally bypassed the parts with the most nutrients—the white membranes next to the peel—forced me to eat the membranes as I cried. Moments later I called my mother to inquire about how I used to eat grapefruit, because the once-felt line separating my authentic behavior from actions inspired by my illness had momentarily vanished. After being reassured that indeed I had always cut grapefruit into triangular segments, I realized that the nurse had been abusive in her position of authority and that I was more mentally intact than I had thought.

*February 26:* Today I feel sick to my stomach. I don't trust my instincts anymore and have lost faith in myself. For the first time in months, my mind went out on me for quite some time. When it happened, I was on the patio smoking and knew I had to get back to my room, which required walking through the common area, where everything seemed surreal. I couldn't figure out if I was at an eldercare facility or a peace rally. People have various theories about why this has happened. Cara told me I was in a manic stage of my depression, while Daniel said that my emotional mind was overpowering my rational mind. Personally, I used to associate this feeling with the self-starvation I'd imposed on my brain. Clearly, it was time to see Dr. Black to get an informed answer.

*February 27:* This morning, for the first time since my admission to the hospital, I saw Dr. Black, who was very warm as he sat by my bedside while I wept. He was extremely encouraging about my potential for overcoming my illness and explained that my mind actually was suffering from mal-nourishment. I think Dr. Black is going to be the person to save me. And although I feel protected in his care, there is still one thing I fear: *What if my body becomes healthier due to nutrients, but my brain does not?*

*February 28:* I have to start seeing the positive in situations. At breakfast, as I looked around the room I couldn't help noticing that most people here are much older than I am. I feel very blessed that at least I have been given the opportunity to deal with my problems at age twenty-one, since after healing, I will have my whole life ahead of me.

Janice gave me a gift today, the well-known Serenity Prayer. This is what I learned from it: I have to accept the things I cannot change, such as the past. I have to find the courage to change the things that I can—for instance, how I choose to live in the present and future. I can spend the rest of my life as a victim or a survivor, and I must understand the difference between the two. Though I cannot control my circumstances, I can control how I let them affect my life. These ideas seem to offer a foundation for real change.

CHAPTER SIX

# A Rebirth in the Making

*Day 18:* Yesterday I overcame a crucial hurdle in the mission to end my self-mutilation: I forced myself to endure the excruciating discomfort of eating three proportional meals. And today I recommitted to the same feat. Like being home with my father, eating to live, as opposed to living to eat or self-starvation, is a test of my ability to leave the past behind and forgive not only others but also myself.

For years I have tried to recall what it was like to eat in a normal fashion and then imitate it, thinking somehow I could turn back the hands of time. It was my fallback formula for attempting to escape the bingeing-then-starving routine I had cultivated, along with an entire repertoire of obsessive-compulsive behaviors, to cope with life's pressures. Finally, in riding out yesterday's distress, which was as much mental as it was physical, I experienced the downside of continually striving to recapture the past. And so I have decided to move forward, with today being the first day of the rest of my life.

Being an obsessive-compulsive perfectionist was a nightmare. Combining the ideas of rigidity and perfectionism results in an extremely uncompromising perspective—an outlook that governed my life in March 1998. I constantly felt disappointed with myself for expending energy on unobtainable goals. And although I left no room for error in my activities, I was, ironically, riddled with flaws. I saw the world in black and white, very seldom enjoying its varied hues. What's more, I had

51

no idea that under such circumstances it is nearly impossible to be happy.

One of my strongest obsessions involved the organization and cleanliness of my surroundings. After spending hours scrubbing my room with antibacterial cleansers, I would notice something out of place and feel suddenly immobilized, as if I'd had the wind knocked out of me. Another major obsession entailed time. I felt as though everything had to be accomplished within a time limit, like sand running through an hourglass. Yet another significant obsession revolved around personal hygiene. I would clip my nails until they bled, pluck my eyebrows into invisibility, scrub my face until it was red and raw, and shower at least four times a day. Adding to the OCD was the sensation I had of always being "dirty" because of my sexual abuse. Not surprisingly, I was eventually given antianxiety medication.

*March 2, 1998:* I am feeling a need to slow down and put a few things in perspective: (1) Striving for perfection only means setting myself up to be let down. No one is perfect, so why should I have to be? (2) The only expectations and limitations in my life are the ones I create myself. (3) I must stop wasting energy on pursuits that are not worth my valuable time—life is too short. Although technically I may always have OCD, I am determined to finally gain control over it.

*March 11:* Today is case conference day. My weight is 78.2 pounds, and it terrifies me to think about hitting 80 pounds.

The meeting went well, and I was granted time out of my room for one and a half hours each night, as well as for Creative Expression class, a group that Karla runs each Thursday. I do not know if it will involve art forms different from those I work with independently in my room, but at least I will be around people.

*March 13:* Today was my first Creative Expression class, attended by six other women. Since the day's topic was self-esteem, we discussed what we liked about ourselves and what others liked about us. Taped to the wall behind each of us was a sheet of paper on which other participants wrote words to describe us. I could not believe what they wrote about me, that I was funny, smart, talented, generous, and positive—perhaps because I read to them. In any case, I am grateful to be sending that kind of energy to others and am sure it comes from an internal source, some aspect of my inner self that was awakened by the work in class. This new ability to transform pain, fear, and hope into words and illustrations is a source of great pride.

*March 14:* What makes me mad about many women in the outside world is that they take drastic measures to stay thin, using laxatives, starving or bingeing and purging after their meals. Most are hypocritical about their behavior, acting like they are naturally slim and being judgmental about people like me. The only difference between me and them is that I got caught and was forced to come out of denial. But at least I am getting help for my eating disorder, while they might spend the rest of their lives in denial.

I am on the verge of a complete meltdown. My thoughts race constantly, and my only relief comes through humming, which alerted the staff to finally put me on antipsychotic medication to slow down my thought processes.

*March 15:* I see two distinct sides to my personality—negative and positive. The negative side seems strong most of the time but is actually very weak. The question is: Am I ready to give up control and comply with the program? My way has not worked for twenty-one years, so it is time to choose something worth struggling for. I can either waste time and energy in a power struggle against the staff or I can work with them to overcome my illness. The real enemy is not the staff but my anorexia. I need to stop holding my body accountable for the abuse, using self-starvation as a means of punishment, and mistrusting the staff. Today is as good a time to start as any. It helps to recall the spiritual experience I had when I tried to commit suicide, especially the words of determination resulting from the vision: "I'm a fighter."

*March 16:* In today's session with Daniel, I started cognitive therapy and was surprised to discover that just because I believe something is true does not make it so. It is amazing how quickly I can make my thoughts more rational once I see how irrational they have been. Obvious examples of my irrational thinking include the following:

- ✳ Jumping to the conclusion that if I get better my family will no longer love me.

- ✳ Overgeneralizing that I will always be anorexic.

- ✳ Blaming myself for my father's sexual abuse.

- ✳ Using emotional reasoning, such as assuming that if I feel fat, I am fat.

*March 20:* I wanted to find a unique way to tell the staff that I was ready to be part of the team. And since I felt I was the only team member facing challenges, I decided to provide *them* with one. So for the March 17 case conference, I gave them two envelopes. The first envelope contained several puzzle pieces and a sheet entitled "Rules of the Game," with the following instructions: "(1) Remove a puzzle piece from the envelope, then pass the envelope on to another team member, continuing until everyone has in his or her possession at least one piece. (2) Work as a team to put the puzzle together. (3) Look at the picture portrayed by the completed puzzle. (4) Now open envelope number two and have someone read the contents aloud."

The picture resembled a clover leaf with a question mark cut out in the center. Drawings and words on the image detailed my history of coping with abuse, including the ways I had punished my body for the sexual abuse and addictions. And folded inside the second envelope was a note that read: "Just as I am the creator of this puzzle, I was also the creator of my self-destructive behaviors. And in the same way you have worked as a team to put together the puzzle, can you work as a team to help me put together the missing puzzle within me for the sake of my future? P.S. The clover is a good-luck charm for our task ahead. Happy St. Patrick's Day!"·

By the time I arrived at the meeting, dressed in my green Snugabye pajamas, the staff was receptive. But I had lost weight that week, and they informed me that they were aware I was exercising. They increased my food consumption again but fortunately did not take away my privileges.

*March 22:* The caloric increase has been extremely difficult on my system. Some nights the kitchen sends me very large portions, probably not realizing that I have to finish what I am served. I am still exercising, but only to build muscles and not to burn calories—or at least that is what I tell myself. I have been manipulating some of my meals, as well, but only because consuming large meals in a short time makes me feel like I am bingeing. I just want to be normal and stop eating once I am full, but I can't or I will be punished.

*March 25:* At the next case conference, I weighed in at my dreaded goal of 80 pounds. For the first time I am excited about my weight gain, because I know it means I will get more privileges. Already I have been awarded a new relaxation class so I can spend some time meditating. My true reward, however, is that I am beginning to view my weight gain positively.

*March 27:* I am starting to feel very confident about my recovery, and my fears are slowly diminishing. Once I begin functioning with positive energy, the real Sara will emerge from behind the mask she has been wearing for a long time. I now see that short-term solutions will never fix long-term problems. Through spiritual work I shall evolve, at which point people will see my inner beauty that has been hidden due to sorrow, addictions, violence, sex, and self-mutilation.

*March 31:* I gained more weight for yesterday's case conference and was awarded two new privileges—I was allowed to go with my mother or Lance to the cafeteria or gift shop, and I was permitted to take a morning walk with Karla, thereby availing myself of an exhilarating option to the recycled air of the hospital.

*April 1:* It is April Fool's Day, but I am no fool because I welcome the challenges my illness has delivered. As Lance tells me, "When one door closes, another opens." I may have been taken away from the outside world, but I am having enlightening experiences here, getting to know my inner self. By contrast, most people go through life not knowing their identity or what they want to accomplish, and some spend their whole life in turmoil, never dealing with their baggage. I have been given the chance to learn about my weaknesses and abilities so I can grow, and I am grateful for this opportunity.

*April 2:* I have chosen a new path—not to be a victim. It all began this morning when Linda suggested I give voice to my anguish by completing a writing exercise about grieving for the many things that were taken from me or destroyed in childhood. While writing about my past, words came to mind such as *lonely, scared, unprotected, sad, violent, disturbing,* and *wrong.* My father, a hot-tempered, critical man, spent most of his time at the office or traveling on business, but when he did come home I was at the mercy of his overwhelming power and control—mentally, emotionally, and sexually. And although I was "Daddy's special little girl," I could never live up to his expectations. To me, his temper symbolized the unjust authority that people can have over others. Since violence became expected, I too learned how to be verbally and physically abusive, not only toward myself but to others as well.

In the process, I lost many of the handholds that guide people through harmonious lives, including my gauge on the parameters of acceptable behavior; my self-esteem, confidence, innocence, pride, and capacity to say no; control over my body; the ability to see intimacy as a pure act of love rather than a dirty ritual; my trust in men; and my view of the world as a beautiful place. I also lost my faith in God and my understanding of others' intentions, my sense of comfort and safety, my belief in unconditional love, and possibly even my life. Further, because we did not communicate, my mother had no way of assuring me a childhood free from harm. I still grieve for lost relationships, opportunities, and time. I also mourn my lost spirit and will to live. When you have never seen the positive side of life, it is difficult to identify anything worth living for.

And yet, it is not too late for rebirth—which I see as a direct outgrowth of having relived my stages of development. My first childhood left me feeling abandoned, neglected, powerless, hurt, angry, in need of perfection, worthless, scared, ashamed, unloved, guilty, and suicidal. By contrast, my second childhood, experienced here in the hospital, brings infusions of support, structure, security, and other nurturing influences.

Through the program, I am starting to develop self-esteem and a sense of being protected, cared for, and helped. Of course, at first, when I had to obey nonnegotiable rules, I also felt frustrated, angry, and rebellious; then I learned to think for myself, be responsible for my actions, have faith in myself, and feel respected, confident, and safe enough to grow. The program is responsible for my rebirth, with the staff standing in as parent figures.

*April 8:* Yesterday's case conference was very productive. I was awarded three new privileges: an extra hour out of my room at night; participation in TAG (Therapeutic Activities Group), a craft-making session led by Karla; and an hour each Tuesday afternoon working out with my trainer, Gretchen. When Karla's around, however, I must remember not to tell Gretchen I have been exercising all this time, though surely she will notice my muscle tone and strength. She'll suspect that my all-consuming passion to remain physically fit has remained unabated. She'll know that my desire for approval, my willingness to seek advice and follow orders, and my attempts to "get with the program" have all succumbed to the force of my relentless obsession with exercise and controlling the only thing I can: my body.

Before our first excursion to the gym, Gretchen decided we should start off in the pool so I could integrate exercise back into my life gradually, through low-impact routines. Although I was excited to start working out officially, putting on the swimsuit my mother brought over made me see that at 90 pounds I was starting to look like a woman again, which I detested. Without visible ribs, slender thighs, and a concave stomach, I could barely face myself in the mirror, let alone expose my body to the public. I spent a week before the pool workout fearful of the worst, but when the day arrived and we had the pool to ourselves, it was an exhilarating experience. Before long, I was in the gym for my hard-won hour per week, weight training with Gretchen, interacting with the public, and feeling normal.

*April 11:* A few hours ago I met another patient suffering from anorexia, but my intuition tells me she is not sincere. Although her need for attention is similar to mine, the intensity of pain is absent, as is the empathy I associate with this illness. For instance, while I was eating she said, "My God, how often do you eat? You know it's all going to catch up with you." Enraged, I barked back, "That's the whole fucking point, bitch." After I told Daniel what happened, we decided I should start assertiveness training. I know how to be aggressive, submissive, manipulative, and passive-aggressive, but not assertive; I have no idea how to express my feelings and ask for what I want in a nonthreatening manner. At first, acting assertively felt like an unnatural way of communicating, but it turned out to be effective and gave me a new sense of confidence and power.

*April 15:* I am proud of myself for being assertive with the other anorexic patient at breakfast this morning. We were sitting at the same table, and this time she made me angry by saying, "I'm going to throw out my food because food makes you fat." So I said, "I feel annoyed when you throw out your food in front of me, claiming food makes you fat, and I would appreciate it if you would keep your inconsiderate comments to yourself and not sit with me at mealtimes." Everyone else at our table clapped, and for the first time since my admission to the hospital, I felt as though I acted in a dignified manner.

Soon, though, my aggression and frustration turned into anger at everyone—the staff, Dr. Black, my father, my mother, and even Lance. I had started to hate their visits because afterward these people could just leave me behind. But I soon realized I was displacing my feelings and that the person I was really angry with was myself. After all, I was the one who had put myself in this situation.

*April 18:* My father came to visit this afternoon, reducing me to tears. He makes me feel like a victim every time I have to look at him. I just want to cry and tell him it wasn't fair, that I was only a child. I wish I had the courage to confront him about all my feelings concerning his abuse. For example, I want to ask him why he molested me, how he could have done that to his own daughter, and if he ever thought about the lifelong consequences of affecting an innocent child's development in this way. I want him to realize that he damaged my self-esteem and brought fear into my world—especially fear of losing control and fear of men.

*April 19:* My feelings toward Dr. Black are ambivalent: I hate and fear him, yet I love and trust him. I don't even want to converse with the staff anymore since it is only a waste of time and energy trying to explain my feelings to them. They argue about my every word, making me feel so alone. The longer I remain a patient, the more I lose faith and trust in the staff, but the staff is also frustrated by the program designed for me, which doesn't seem to be working.

*April 23:* At the case conference two days ago, I was awarded three new privileges, or more accurately, two privileges and one punishment: (1) more time out of my room, (2) interaction with the staff if I need to talk with someone when my emotions are running high, and (3) Anger Management class. What the staff really should have said was that they would now be watching my every move, making me feel claustrophobic by their presence.

· As it turned out, I attended only a few Anger Management classes, since being in a group with ten angry individuals was only adding fuel to my own fire. I did learn, however, that I needed to start taking responsibility for my anger and that no one can make us feel an emotion we do not choose to feel.

In addition, while I am doing better at not manipulating my food, I'm extremely phobic about reaching 100 pounds. Most anorexics have a phobia about weight gain, each having reasons of their own. The following are a few of my reasons: (1) Since I have a distorted body image, I already feel overweight, so asking me to gain weight would be like asking a 400-pound woman to gain another 20 pounds. (2) The discomfort within my body and the fact that I cannot control how I gain weight make me feel violated. (3) Death sometimes looks better than the mental torture I am enduring. (4) Gaining weight means becoming a woman again, and due to my extreme vulnerability I do not feel secure as a woman. I feel protected at 65 pounds, since no one would want to rape or abuse a person who looks ill. Too often, I forget that rape is not about sensuality but rather a crime of hate, rage, control, and violence. And in these times of forgetfulness I hope no man will find me attractive, a prospect that enables me to avoid the pressure, or obligation, of intercourse. (5) I do not want to lose my family's love, and I am aware that they pay more attention to me when I am anorexic.

*April 25:* Yesterday was my three-month anniversary and a day of rebellion. With no one to stop me, I almost made it outdoors. Still, I know the day I run out of here I will ultimately die since I need the treatment here to survive.

I did not eat my snacks today and decided to be honest about it. Considering how hard I have been following the program lately, I felt sure the staff would understand, but instead they assured me there would be consequences.

*April 27:* Today was case conference day. Now that I am close to 100 pounds, the staff says there is no retreating. I tried to walk out, but Dr. Black made me go back to my room. I decided to act as though I wanted to play by their rules, but secretly I am manipulating calories, exercising twice the amount allowed, and storing the bottles of water they let me buy at the gym. In the days to come, my weight will be almost solely from water and my thoughts will be kept to myself. If this plan does not work, I am determined to escape.

## CHAPTER SEVEN

# Dying to Memories

$\mathcal{D}$*ay 25:* Last night I dreamed that I died. I was running through a drizzly, dense forest toward a destination I could not see but thought of as a distant finish line. When at last I reached my journey's end, my trembling knees and aching muscles collapsed beneath me, and enshrouded in darkness, I fell to the ground, dead. Then the blackness all around me began shimmering with pinpoints of light as I drifted toward the hereafter. I was startled to discover that an existence of any sort, much less a bright and multihued one, awaited me beyond the finish line. Clearly, this dream reflects my current efforts to bring closure to the past and transition to a future of potential.

Unfortunately the same cannot be said about my ambiguous living arrangement. Conversations with my father are only about my father. When he is not obsessively seeking a rationale for his past behaviors, he gushes with sorrow over his "immoral and unlawful activity." He won't discuss current events with me, or the weather, or even town gossip. So on the one hand while I intend to forgive him, on the other I refuse to appease his soul from the vantage point of victim. He will have to earn my trust in him.

I suspect this will emerge over time. Already, even though I keep the door separating our living quarters securely locked at night, I feel an anomalous sense of comfort when he is in the house. When he goes away on business, the noises of the house keep me hyperalert. In an ironic turn of events, the man who used to terrify me now has me feeling protected and secure.

The stress I was under in the spring of 1998 caused me to have horrible dreams. I would wake up each night crying but with no memory of the precipitating events, just a petrifying sense of familiarity eating away at the core of my being. At times, startled by the male attendants doing their night checks, I would yell at them to get out of my fuckin' room. More often, I would simply stay in bed sobbing for hours, confused, frustrated, and exasperated about my inability to recall the elusive dream. Distraught by the disconnection from this heavily guarded portion of myself, I would pummel my mind with questions—*What have I been conjuring up in the sinister darkness of night? By not recalling my dream, am I missing a significant premonition? Or are these spells the result of an overactive imagination driving me at full throttle?*—aching to know the answers. What I really wanted was control over my dreams.

Around this time, my body started to change in eerie ways. Prepubescent breasts began emerging, as well as a thin layer of insulation covering my ribs, stomach, and face. The comfort in emaciation I had worked so hard to achieve was slipping away, for I persistently felt dizzy and on the verge of exploding internally. While attempting to swallow food, I would gag, and after completing a meal I'd feel nauseous. I wanted to run away from my body, which was shutting down so rapidly I felt certain that very soon I would no longer be able to talk or move.

*May 8, 1998:* Today is my birthday. I asked the staff not to deliver the cake they usually give to patients on such occasions, then I went to spend the day with Daniel, opening up to him. We discussed my father's split nature—the violence and fear-based control tactics he exercised during my childhood and his passivity and generosity over the past decade. I acknowledged that my father was abusive, aware that Daniel understood the term to refer to verbal, emotional, and also sexual abuse. We also talked about my mother's hardened and cold disposition, and my desire for her to display the love and affection I've so needed from her. Daniel offered no feedback but rather clarified my disclosures and gently probed sensitive areas, making sure I remained in control of the conversation.

Something must have come unplugged, because for days afterward I was flooded with memories. They centered on two subjects: the physiological reflexes I experienced upon hearing my father's footsteps in the hallway and while undergoing the forced oral sex. Talking about these menacing memories helped me identify present-day correlates they were most likely triggering. My anxiety attacks, for example, seemed rooted in an almost cellular memory of the approaching footsteps, while my gagging appeared associated with the oral sex. In fact, I realized that the full spectrum of my eating and drinking difficulties probably emanated from the oral distress I endured repeatedly in childhood.

*May 12:* At my case conference this morning, my weight registered a little higher, thanks to the water, but not enough. I'm already hiding as many bottles as possible, and I'm worried the staff will find out what I've been doing. I received no new privileges today; in fact, Dr. Black said that if my weight drops I will lose the ones I already have. He wants me to try a form of hypnotherapy that utilizes a drug to decrease inhibitions, hoping it might help me unblock more of my sexual abuse memories. I refused, unwilling to put myself in a situation where I have no control, with a man I don't trust. He seemed to respect my readiness to stand up for myself. He also understood that I was just trying to find peace, not attempting to rebel against the program.

*May 16:* While walking with Karla this afternoon, I asked her the question that has been foremost on my mind: "How much longer can they hold me here?" Hesitantly she replied, "Sara, you're a voluntary patient." I had no idea I was voluntary—I could not recall signing admission forms—and could hardly believe that all this time I thought I was here against my will. Then Karla added, "Though if you had tried to leave when first admitted, they would have made you involuntary." I'm now faced with a big decision: Do I leave and go back to life as an anorexic, and perhaps die, or do I stay and receive the mental help I desperately need in order to recover? I suppose I'll stay until I see further signs telling me to definitely give up.

*May 19:* Linda thinks I'm in a big rut and that to get moving I need a taste of life. So today I asserted myself and told Dr. Black that I need passes to the outside world. I was awarded one pass per weekend, allowing me four to six hours in the company of Lance, who was chosen because of his dedication to my recovery.

Lance is everything to me—my angel, strength, motivation, and inspiration. Knowing it is important symbolically for me to watch things grow, he has brought me a new plant every week, and on my birthday a houseplant as big as a tree. Mom brought new pots and soil to make sure they flourish. Lance has also helped *me* grow, giving me, among other things, a Talmudic quote I posted above my bed: "Every blade of grass has its angel who bends over and whispers, 'Grow, grow.'"

As it turned out, I cherished our time together, going to trendy cafés for tea and for walks downtown along the river, and I always felt sad when it ended. Once, when he was late, I cried, because I was sure he had forgotten about me. Other times, despite my feelings of love and appreciation, I would lash out at him verbally and push him away, selfishly testing his loyalty—only to discover that he loved me unconditionally. I felt a similar love from my mother and Janice, though less so from Jackie, who rarely showed her emotions.

This pattern of distrust among our family members had been established long before. When I was sixteen and first discussed my abuse, for example, Jackie did not want to hear what my father had done to me, and my mother said I was so dishonest that no one knew if they could trust my word. Because I needed my family to fill in details I could not remember and wanted the abuse to stop being a shameful secret, their lack of trust further increased my sense of isolation and diminished my self-esteem. A portion of my treatment therefore involved learning how to better understand and relate to them, and how to maintain a sense of self-worth independent of the opinions of others. The goal was to start feeling good from the inside out.

At the same time, I had to learn to accept others for being themselves rather than how I thought they should be. Insisting that my mother and Jackie evolve into demonstrably affectionate human beings prevented me from seeing the many subtle ways in which they loved and supported me.

*May 24:* It is my four-month anniversary and something within me is coming to a head, fueled in part by an unexpected visit from my father.

Seeing him, all I could do was scream, "Get the hell out of here!" It felt powerful to vent my anger toward the right person for once and to see its effect—fear in his eyes.

*May 26:* By the time of today's case conference, the tables had again turned. My weight was down, causing the staff to decree that in my situation, weight gains will henceforth take priority over mental well-being. I tried to explain that I needed mental relief in order to reach 100 pounds, but they gave me an ultimatum: either I agree to follow the program or I leave AMA (against medical advice). For me, following the program was not an option; indeed, asking an anorexic to willingly gain weight is like asking a priest to willingly worship the devil. Consequently, I called Lance and asked him to take me home. Aware that I was still very ill and possibly suicidal, Lance could not understand why I was permitted to leave, and he asked to speak with Dr. Black, who explained that when and if I could agree to their terms I was welcome to come back for treatment. Lance told me that he could not transport me until much later in the day, hoping perhaps that with time to think, I would change my mind. Instead, I called Tammy to pick me up and told Lance to meet me at my mother's house. As I walked out the hospital door, Cara looked at me and said earnestly, "Don't let your pride stand in the way of coming back."

*May 28:* The last forty-eight hours have been like a bad dream. By the time Lance arrived at my mother's house, I was having one anxiety attack after another, so he drove me around the rest of the day and most of the night, thinking that if he left me alone in this state of hopelessness, I would probably commit suicide. He was most likely right, for I felt unable to function or even make simple decisions on my own.

Finally, I told Lance I wanted to go back to the hospital—a request he promptly fulfilled. But when we reached the door I froze, unable to move. Lance went in to talk with the nurses then returned with Cara, who carried out my night snack in case I was hungry. Looking back and forth from her to Lance, I promised to talk to Dr. Black in the morning and, until then, cause myself no harm.

It was evening before I could see Dr. Black. Once in his office, I broke

down, telling him I could not yet make it on my own and was ready to follow the program. Returning to my room, I felt safe at last.

I weighed in today at 94.7 pounds without manipulating the scales
through water consumption, and I ate all of my meals. Maybe I have
changed.

*May 29:* Dr. Maguire, who was notified only when physical intervention
became necessary, would often come by as time allowed her to. Today, she
managed to stop by between rounds to assure me she would always be on
my side. She said that if I feel the program here is not working, she will
make other arrangements for me on the outside. I thanked her, well aware
that I am not ready to throw away the months of work I have done here.

*June 4:* Within days of returning to the hospital, I was back to my old ways,
though with more intensity. I was throwing out more food than I was eating, exercising twice as much as before, and drinking water by the liter. My
obsession with personal hygiene had also veered out of control: I showered
at every opportunity and attempted to shave each hair on my body, from
the neck down. Thoughts raced through my mind, and I could hear voices
cruelly saying that I am fat, lazy, dirty, and not worthy of food. They
advised me to eat less, exercise more, and lose weight, asserting that I
deserved to be alone and starve to death.

Because of the voices, Dr. Black increased my medication, but my
questions about possible consequences all go unanswered. What I find
frustrating about this psychiatric unit is that if you request to be educated
about the medication you are taking, you first need a doctor's permission,
and once that's been secured the staff may fail to tell you about such side
effects as increased appetite and weight gain. Voluntary or involuntary, I
believe it is an individual's right to know about the effects of medications
that are prescribed.

*June 18:* The June 9 case conference, while far from pleasant, proved to be
an adventure I will never forget. Dr. Black immediately laid down the law,
declaring that from now on I had to eat with a staff member present and
that my door had to be open at all times, which meant no exercising.

When he finished, I stared teary-eyed at the team then, dazed and bewildered, drifted out of the room. Interpreting his edicts as a sign for me to give up, I packed a small bag and, intending to leave again, wrote a note:

> *To the team and my family: I am at a loss for words. I am sorry for giving up and failing you. I am too tired to fight anymore. I want to rest and find peace. I will never be able to express what you mean to me—your support and love have been a most precious gift. I love you with all my heart and soul. Keep up the fight against anorexia. I failed the system, it didn't fail me. Here are my journals from day one; hopefully they will provide you with insight into this illness and help you understand how it has affected me. The final journal will be with me and will sum up the rest of my struggle. Know that this is what will make me happy and bring me peace at last. I will always be with you in spirit. I love you. Sara*

I waited until the nurses were busy handing out the morning medications and then walked calmly out the door. I was halfway across the parking lot, almost home free, when I heard one of the attendants yell, "Sara, stop!" With my adrenaline pumping, I ran out of the parking lot, across four lanes of traffic, and hid inside a McDonald's dumpster until I was sure no one was searching the area. Next I went to the mall, took a cash advance on my credit card, and proceeded to the drugstore, where I managed to buy six boxes of sleeping pills without anyone questioning my motives. From there, I took a taxi several miles out of town to a seedy motel, where I was certain no one would think to look for me. I paid for a week's stay in advance and asked for no disturbances, telling the owner I was completing a novel.

Within hours, I had nearly completed the final chapter of my life story when the police arrived at my door. I had been reported missing, and following Lance's intuition they were searching every motel and hotel in the area. I flashed on Dr. Black, and how my suicide note would reward him with the necessary ammunition to petition changing my voluntary status to involuntary. Gasping for breath, I begged the officers not to take me back, but take me back they did, since they were the ones in control.

Upon my return, I was told to put on my pajamas, get into bed, and

## Dr. Black's Certificate Petitioning My Commitment
## As an Involuntary Patient

*Facts observed by me:*

Well-known to me over 3 years. Has severe anorexia nervosa (weight down to 68 lbs. recently). Very depressed, hopeless, writing and verbally expressing suicidal drive in the face of feeling that she can neither forgive nor tolerate regression in weight. Left hospital 2 days ago—lost 5 lbs. in 24 hours and asked for readmission. Has stated her intent to die.

*The nature or degree of the mental disorder suffered by the person is as follows:*

Severe anorexia nervosa, depression, and posttraumatic stress disorder.

*The reasons for my opinion that the person to whom this certificate relates is not mentally competent to give or refuse to give consent in relation to routine clinical medical treatment are as follows:*

She knows what she needs to do in terms of meds, refeeding to gain, observation while eating, but due to overwhelming anxiety and self-loathing for normalizing her weight, she would prefer to die than tolerate the temporary distress. She has been informed of the transient nature of the distress, but refuses treatment, while at the same time saying that what she is doing is irrational. She weighs 97 lbs. and is malnourished, with distorted body image.

*In my opinion, the request is in the best interest of the person in relation to whom the order is sought because:*

☀ Compliance with inpatient Rx program carries at least a 75 percent likelihood of recovery, if she gains beyond her phobic weight.

☀ She has repeatedly demonstrated over the past year a pattern of profound weight loss, to life-threatening levels, when not in a treatment program.

☀ Discontinuing treatment is of far less risk than death by suicide.

☀ We have tried voluntary Rx for past 4 months, [but she has] now escaped from hospital, intending to kill herself.

*Figure 1*

prepare for an injection to help me relax. Its effect was more than relaxing, prompting me to nickname the medication the KOD, the "knockout drug." It made me sleep for three days straight, slip in and out of sleep for four more days, then stumble through another series of days dealing with aftereffects similar to those of a bad hangover. In moments of flickering semiconsciousness, I was instructed to eat but did so with great difficulty, due to an adverse reaction to the injection that made it hard for me to swallow, talk, or even breathe. My mother came to visit and was horrified to see me so heavily sedated. Lance visited too, showing his characteristic faith in my future while talking about a narrative he presumed I would one day compose by weaving together my journal entries. "This is not how it ends, Sara," he said with a twinkle in his eye. "Many chapters have yet to be written."

As I suspected, Dr. Black filled out the paperwork requesting that I be made an involuntary patient (see figure 1). My hearing was set for June 16, which also was the day of my next case conference. The time leading up to these events was like the calm before a storm. When your psychiatrist petitions your change in status from voluntary to involuntary, you are represented by a patient advocate at the hearing, which you yourself need not attend. And because I chose not to attend the proceedings and my advocate had a thick French accent, I could barely understand the discussion that had ensued in my absence. The advocate's final words, however, were all too clear: "Sara, you are now involuntary for the next thirty days. I'm sorry it did not go the way you wished."

That night, Dr. Black came to my room with another announcement: "Sara, we are placing you in CNC." CNC stands for concentrated nursing care, which I soon found out was a fancy name for solitary confinement.

## CHAPTER EIGHT

# IN A PRISON of MY OWN MAKING

*Day 32:* At age twenty-four, I live a life of solitude. The only time the phone rings is when my mother calls; everyone else I have shut out due to my fears of rejection. Even calls from my mother, however, can impact negatively on my self-image, especially if I am reminded of the time twelve years ago when she said she was unable to love me. Nor is there solace interacting with my father, who, bypassing the abuse, routinely refers to his inadequacies as a father.

My father's obsessions, however, are actually clarifying for me. Despite his failure to see beyond the victim within me, I am learning that I am not victimized but rather free to make many choices regarding my future existence. And I fully intend to exercise my options by breaking out of this isolation and inviting human interactions. I'd like to start by reestablishing contact with my family members, who represent the few souls that have remained unconditionally by my side. It is in times of crisis that we realize who our true allies are, and now, one month into this sojourn in my father's house, I can see that even this man, in addition to my mother, Lance, and Janice, has never faltered as one of my greatest supporters.

CNC was hell. My room consisted of cement walls, a mattress on the floor, and a wooden door with a small window toward the top. Immediately after arriving, I kicked and punched the walls. Chris, the attendant, tried to calm me down but quickly resorted to an injection, a faster-acting sedative than the one I had received eight days before. I was given strict orders to stay in bed 24/7, but I told them exactly where they could stick their rules. While not sleeping or being forced to eat, I exercised. At first, I was not allowed visits even from my immediate family or access to my journal. Nor was I permitted to have books, music, or cigarettes, and the nicotine withdrawal added to my rage. Worse, the staff watched me while I used the washroom and as I ate my meals.

On my second day in CNC, when Cara brought my breakfast I threw the food against the wall. All day I was verbally abusive, viewing the nurses as guards and Dr. Black as the warden. During one fit of rage, eight security people came to deal with all 95 pounds of me. I actually enjoyed fighting them, taking out my anger and frustration by kicking, punching, and biting them as they hurled me around the room. Finally, I tied a string from my pajamas around my neck, but the security people showed up and rescued me before it had cut off my circulation. Next they stripped me, exposing and degrading me as one of the men, seeming to take pleasure in removing my pajamas, whistled. Adding to my misery was the fact that the heating system did not work, causing me to shiver, so I exercised in the nude and, anytime the nurses came in to check on me, made futile attempts to escape.

On the third day, I was again allowed to wear my pajamas. Eating was no problem; I even began sneaking extra food as a demonstration of control, since Dr. Black had stated that I was allowed to consume only what they specified. That night, my father came to visit me. I had asked him to sneak in a chocolate bar for me, a request he reported to the staff. I was enraged that he couldn't keep this little secret when for twenty-two years I had been keeping his secret about abusing me. The horror of my past came out in front of some of the nurses as I screamed the words *sex, incest, hand jobs, blow jobs, molestation,* and *rape.* Having finally managed to confront him after years of lacking the necessary courage, I hoped he would admit to what he had done and apologize. But instead he gave me two alternatives: I could either go to court and put him in jail or take back what I had said, telling the nurses I had lied. Moments later, he asked briskly, "Okay, if it's true, then how big is my penis?" whereupon the nurses kicked him out. In retrospect, I can't help but wonder how long he had been rehearsing that speech, dreading the day I would expose him.

I could not imagine why people who had raped or killed received more privileges than me. It made no sense that I was locked up while my father reveled in freedom. Life had never seemed more cruel and unfair. My only solace was the thought of reaching 100 pounds in two to three weeks so I too could be free—discharged from this mortifying confinement in CNC.

*June 23, 1998:* Another case conference day has come. I have gained weight, so I am allowed four ten-minute supervised smoking breaks per day.

This morning, Dr. Black made his disapproval of my exercising crystal clear. I told him it's essential, that I use it to pass the time and vent my anger and frustration. He replied that the purpose of CNC is to keep me from harming myself and that exercising obsessively is detrimental to my well-being.

Dr. Maguire, stopping by later, raised concerns about Dr. Black's treatment methods, showing me that at least one person was on my side. Even so, I am acutely aware of the craziness of my actions and that the ugly part of me that is shining through. And while I understand that extreme situations call for drastic solutions, I am also aware that such solutions can provoke intense reactions in individuals forced to deal with them.

Some of the staff, indicating that under similar circumstances they would be able to control their behavior, appear self-righteous. I doubt they have been trained to deal with the effects of a patient's seclusion, which can be intensely traumatizing. Many well-documented cases show the extremes people will go to when faced with life-threatening isolation, such as those Piers Paul Read describes in his book *Alive: The Miracle of the Andes,* in which survivors of a plane crash are forced into cannibalism as a means of enduring. While the comparison may seem exaggerated, I feel every bit as lost in a seclusion room, naked and deprived of my dignity, as a plane crash victim lost in the barren wild. My fear, pain, and overwhelming desire not to succumb to the elements are just as real. Moreover, I am judged harshly every day, an equally difficult situation to deal with.

*June 24:* This morning I told Daniel I was sure Dr. Black had no clue how to treat individuals with anorexia. I feel anger toward him and the rest of the staff, though mostly I'm feeling hurt, because I thought they would help me but instead they betrayed and neglected me. I also told Daniel how much more obsessed I have become about suicide since the transfer. Indeed, I am exercising eight more hours a day and have started writing a day in advance in my journal. I can't help but wonder if it's necessary to experience abuse in order to recover from abuse.

Looking back, I see that my angry and hurt feelings toward Dr. Black were due to the psychoanalytic phenomenon known as transference, which occurs when patients react to their therapist in the same way they would to a pivotal figure from their childhood. In my case, although displeased with Dr. Black's treatment methods, I had also displaced onto him the emotions I felt toward my father. This gave me opportunities to safely express the anger directed at my father, rather than continuing to express it internally.

*June 26:* Today I told Daniel how liberating it is to no longer carry the burden of my secret and that in addressing it I had overcome a huge obstacle. What I felt but didn't tell him was that I no longer experience shame and humiliation while speaking about being sexually abused. In confronting my father, I have shifted the guilt to the responsible party. Now all I ask is that he accept responsibility for his actions.

My father asked if he could talk to me tonight, so out of curiosity I said yes. But what a fool I am! As before, he tried to convince me that my memories are only dreams. Determined to never again question the truth, I told him to leave, explaining that until he can acknowledge what he's done I no longer have a father.

*June 28:* One good thing about CNC is that it has taken away my distractions. Now I invest nearly all my time and energy in exercising and focusing on my issues. I have decided to work on the following problems by myself: (1) body image, (2) weight and food phobia, (3) PTSD, (4) anger, verbal abuse, and physical violence, (5) thoughts and behaviors related to sexuality, (6) OCD, (7) perfectionism, (8) negative thoughts and feelings, and (9) lack of self-esteem and self-love. I need to turn this beast into a beauty.

*June 30:* Today is case conference day. I gained 1.2 pounds this past week and was given the new privilege of three additional smoking breaks.

Also, my father called, telling Linda that he truly didn't remember sexually abusing me but that he has started having a few dreamlike memories. Maybe he really doesn't remember, but it isn't my job to help him through his flashbacks. I can't let him interfere with my recovery.

A new patient moved in next door, and Dr. Black does not want us conversing through the wall. She is extremely overweight—a compulsive eater. Such a gross habit is beyond my comprehension. I may have compulsions of my own, but at least I have willpower and will never be fat. Looking back, I can say I'm now a firm believer in two healthier concepts: there is no excuse for ignorance and through karma we learn profound lessons. Because of karma, the energy driving the outcomes of our actions, what we put out is what we later receive. I hope I can use these beliefs to make my future more positive.

*July 7:* It is case conference day and I now weigh 97 pounds. I was awarded five extra minutes on each of my seven ten-minute breaks, but my food consumption was also increased. My status for being voluntary or involuntary is coming up for review on July 16. I know in my heart that if I were to leave I would rather die than live the tortured life of an anorexic. I hope I am made involuntary so I will be forced to complete my treatment. I am so confused; one minute I want out of here, and the next I want to stay. What I'd really like is to stay in the hospital but be let out of this hostile CNC environment.

After being institutionalized for a period of time, you feel safe because you know what to expect. Sheltered from taking responsibility, you do not have to live in the world as an adult making important decisions and dealing with the stresses of everyday life. After a while you become dependent on the system, but recovery should be about empowering an individual rather than making the person dependent.

I've recently been allowed to read up on topics related to my illness. The catch is that the printed information has to be delivered by a staff member, which I view as another form of control. I read about PTSD and flashbacks, phobias, OCD, self-esteem, and most intriguingly, body image, which helps me alter the way I view myself. I realize that the way I see myself is not how the rest of the world sees me and needs to be changed. I see myself as a feeble victim of circumstance, when really I am imprisoned in my own thoughts of incompetence.

So I took a few small steps today toward changing my self-image by writing a letter to my body, stating how I've abused it and acknowledging all that it has done for me nonetheless. In conclusion, I looked down at my body, crying for the harm I caused it, and wrote:

> *I have proved that I am incapable of treating you with the love and respect you are worthy of receiving. I didn't even give you the love and compassion I would give to a friend. You were not the enemy; I was. I now live with guilt, shame, and regret for your misfortune. Please forgive me.*
>
> *My deepest apologies and love,*
> *Sara*

*July 13:* I can't believe that my water intake has to be accounted for. I am allowed only one small glass of water and one cup of herbal tea per meal—amounting, over the course of a day, to about half the water a person is required to drink. After feeling dehydrated from exercising and the summer's heat, I discovered I could drink extra water in the shower. Although a staff member is in the room with me when I shower, the curtain is drawn, so she cannot see me.

I talked to Dr. Black today, and he said that as long as I am still not menstruating I am not healthy and that if I refuse to go over 100 pounds, which I will, there must be consequences for my actions. He added that my father had been calling him and had even sent letters, which I will be permitted to read when I am ready. Although curious about the content, I am determined not to allow my father's manipulative nature to interfere with my recovery.

*July 14:* Today is case conference day and I just squeaked by at 98 pounds. Eve is increasing my calories. I told Daniel that my decision to stop at 100 pounds is based on a refusal to set myself up for a cycle of dieting once I leave. He said I should tell Dr. Black I deserve to be rewarded for reaching my phobic weight since it's a great accomplishment—if not for him, at least for me.

*July 16:* My involuntary status was officially renewed for another thirty days. The new patient advocate who represented me at the tribunal, Angie, appears to be in her early forties and anorexic, though she manages to keep her weight at a level safe enough to avoid hospitalization. Even so, she has a distorted body image, wants desperately to lose more weight, and eats to please others—adding up to a life with no quality or enjoyment. If this is what I have to look forward to, I would rather die. I wonder if anorexia nervosa is like alcoholism: once an anorexic, always an anorexic. On the bright side, Leah reminded me that no two people are alike, and Dr. Black offered to find me a recovered anorexic as a positive role model.

Kayla, an eating disorders specialist, asked me where I thought people suffering from an eating disorder get the idea that anorexia nervosa is incurable. "From society, TV shows, and professionals," I answered. Broadcasting networks are in the habit of showcasing emaciated individuals on the brink of death, who rarely appear to recover from their misfortune. As for professionals, a nurse once told me I would probably spend the rest of my life with this illness and therefore needed to learn how to cope. Even Dr. Black, who considers it curable, has documented that I have only a 75 percent chance of recovery, a statistic I was given while quite ill. To most people such odds may sound encouraging, but to me it's horrifying to have a one-in-four chance of remaining this way forever. Society, TV shows, and professionals need to start sending messages of hope not despair.

I asked Daniel why I developed anorexia. He explained that it was most likely the result of different factors, including a desire for control over my body (because I didn't have it while my father was sexually abusing me), self-hate (punishing myself for my father's mistakes and feeling unworthy), not wanting to be a woman (feeling unsafe and not trusting men), and perfectionism (especially regarding body fat, or a less-than-flawless physique).

Lately, because of my propensity to engage in ritualistic acts of exercise and self-starvation, I've become caught in a vicious cycle: Eve raises my calories, I exercise for an extra hour, Eve raises my calories again, and I exercise more. With the amount of food I'm currently eating, however, there is not enough time in the day for exercising sufficiently to avoid gaining weight. I am so obsessed with maximizing my exercise time that I have stopped taking my full fifteen-minute breaks. And isolation has caused me to become so phobic of social interactions that when I do take breaks I sit alone. I have even started turning away from my family when they visit during one of the eleven hours in which I exercise.

*July 21:* On this case conference day, the scale shows I have gained .5 pounds. Eve once again increased my calories, but she is allowing me one glass of water with my nighttime snack. Jackie visited today, showing how much she really does care about me, and in fact always has. She even sat with me in my room, a courageous act for someone so claustrophobic. When visitors come, the staff usually allows my door to be open, but when Jackie was here a fight broke out in the corridor and they shut my door, much to her dismay.

*July 24:* This is my six-month anniversary. I have been told that I'm setting records for the length of time anyone has been in treatment here, but my illness is very complicated. Dr. Black said that he will allow me to maintain 100 pounds for a couple of weeks before gaining more weight. What he doesn't know is that I will never see 101 pounds. After his visit, I think I had a psychotic breakdown, because I laughed, danced, and sang at the top of my lungs—when I wasn't crying.

The confinement is driving me to insanity. This evening I snapped at my night nurses. Eve had apparently forgotten to write orders for my glass of water, so Amy and Chris would not bring me any with my snack. Choking down a bran muffin with peanut butter and not water drove me to distraction. I called Amy a bitch and Chris a bastard, and they in turn called me abusive, which made me aware that I am just like my father—the person I hate most in this world. I have become so desensitized to the humiliating, harmful words used by society that I no longer realize how degrading they are. I must not become immune to abuse and violence, but rather see them as bad viruses that must be continually fought. Perhaps Amy and

Chris had reason to distrust my request for water since I had often lied about what I did with it. The situation reminds me of the childhood story "The Boy Who Cried Wolf"; if you lie about something habitually, you can't expect to be believed when you later tell the truth about it.

*July 26:* Gail, a new nurse working tonight, said she had been warned that I was manipulative, while the nurse on duty last week called me hateful, due to my refusal to eat grapefruit at lunch a few months back. I can't believe the monster I have become; I must be the most detested patient here. It is no wonder I was cursed with anorexia, for I am unworthy of food. They would probably all be happier if I were dead, which is exactly what I deserve.

Being called bad names makes me think I'm bad. And bad people often do bad things just to prove who they are. A secure identity, albeit a negative one, is often better than a tenuous identity. I think negative adjectives like *manipulative, hateful, rude,* and so forth truly suck when they apply to people fighting for their lives. Hell, wouldn't you manipulate people if the alternative was death or a slow torture completely out of your control?

Actually, they don't *all* view me as a bad person. Some have said they consider my behavior partly a reaction to confinement, partly an effect of anorexia, and partly due to my past sexual abuse, while others have suggested possible personality disorder. This makes me see that what's bad is not me as a person but rather my behavior. I also know that although they have diminished my self-esteem by dwelling on my negative traits, they simply want me to take responsibility for my actions.

Treating patients with respect, empathy, and understanding will make them feel less threatened. As a result, they are likely to be less aggressive and more apt to compromise and engage in a treatment plan. Positive reinforcement brings positive change.

*July 28:* At today's case conference, my weight was the same as last week (98.5 pounds), and consequently Dr. Black instructed Eve to increase my calories again. He can be insensitive at times. For example, he walked by while I was eating lunch and mentioned the "big day" coming up—when

I reach 100 pounds. Then he commented on the liquid meal substitute I am expected to complete in addition to my meal, saying, "That will do the body good." I felt as though he was deliberately trying to increase my anxiety. Then I wondered if all my anguish over possibly reaching 100 pounds could really be a form of grieving for my anorexic self and that later I will accept the change. In any case, I am tired of the constant power struggles between me and Dr. Black, due to his arrogant treatment of me. Any battle should be against my illness, not each other.

I realize, too, that the worst kind of anger is misplaced rage and that my ambivalent feelings toward Dr. Black resemble those I have toward my father. Moreover, I am angry with my family for allowing Dr. Black to cage me in CNC, though I understand the helplessness a family must experience when one of them is classified as involuntary (see page 167 for a parental perspective).

So desperate am I to gain control of my life that I have started playing a game: the object is to see if I can manipulate calories during mealtime while under supervision. So at dinner I dropped a utensil on the floor, and while the nurse was picking it up I spit my Brussels sprouts into my napkin. As insignificant as such an act may be, it made me feel like I still had the power of choice.

*August 3:* Today may be my last day of sanity, because tomorrow is D-Day, when I reach 100 pounds. I fear I may go crazy, but perhaps they will use the KOD, the knockout drug, on me. I wonder what reaching 100 pounds will actually prove, since mentally I am still anorexic. I feel overwhelmed after six and a half months, gaining 30-plus pounds, shedding many tears, and fighting numerous physical and psychological battles. I pray for the strength and courage to look at tomorrow as a victory, not a defeat.

I wept for a little girl newly admitted to CNC. Hearing her scream as the men stripped her, I could feel her anger and humiliation. I cried for myself as well, because I knew it could happen to me again.

*August 4:* On this case conference day, I weighed 100.4 pounds. I received no new privileges, but was told I would when my mood stabilizes. Dr. Black said he wanted me to start eating with the rest of the group. This seems degrading, coming out of the "hole" to eat massive amounts of food in front of strangers.

At first, I felt numb, but later I cried and vented my anger by yelling. Finally, I realized two things: (1) 100 is just a number, since I feel no different than I did at 95 pounds, and (2) I am distraught by the prospect of actually dealing with my issues and normalizing my life. Only later did I learn that a key step in recovery is to stop focusing on the big picture and begin living one day at a time.

*August 6:* As outrageous as it sounds, I'm going to miss CNC. The rooms, during my time here, have all been occupied by girls, and the nurses call us the "Chain Gang" or the "CNC Spice Girls." I'm probably a combination of Sporty Spice and Scary Spice. I feel protected and safe here, and at times the attendants seem like my best friends: Leah has brought love and laughter, and made me paper sunflowers, symbols of health and potential; I can converse with Dean on a deep level, since his brother committed suicide and he listens with compassion; Don reads to me from the paper as he supervises my morning meal, keeping me informed on current events. The funniest night was when Don, a man in his fifties, tried to do one of my yoga poses and Leah appeared, breaking into laughter. James, who takes me for my first cigarette of the morning, wraps us up in blankets so tight that we have to hop with both feet together to get outside.

Today I took a step forward by eating in the day room, although in my mind I planned to cut back my calories by 1,000 per day, or 7,000 per week, the equivalent of two pounds. Eating in the day room wasn't as bad as I assumed it would be, since I was still closely supervised and therefore didn't have to face the other people alone. While venturing into public places I still want to be guarded by the staff and simply can't be by myself. I must be either insane or scared, or both, because I told Dr. Black that if I in fact become voluntary on August 16 chances are I will leave and, feeling overwhelmed, take my life. Dr. Black replied that he had already planned to renew my involuntary status for sixty days and needed a second opinion from another psychiatrist on the unit, Dr. Adams. Fortunately Dr. Black had me talk to Dr. Adams back in June, so he knows my history.

*August 7:* A spot weigh-in this morning showed I had lost 2 pounds, which doesn't make sense according to my calculations. Then tonight I enjoyed a visit from my grandparents, whom I hadn't seen since my sister's wedding. The best part of the visit was when my grandfather gave me one of his famous bear hugs. Maybe being healthy will bring blessings and not the curses I have predicted. I must stop making assumptions about the future and live in the present, the only reality I can know.

*August 8:* This morning I made an attempt to escape, but failed. Each morning, part of my breakfast is an untoasted bagel, so Don usually asks Judy, the day therapy nurse, to heat it up. This time Judy complained loudly about how tired she was of catering to me, and that I should be warming the bagels myself but am not allowed to. Don, who noticed I was crying, said, "Sara, everyone is just really frustrated." I assumed the source of their frustration was me, and not the program.

Later, during my cigarette break, I sobbed to Karla about being a burden to the staff and feeling impatient with my illness, for which there is no quick cure. Suddenly, overcome with hopelessness and wanting to erect walls so the staff would all give up on me, I ran. Karla yelled a code as she chased after me, then Don and Diane eventually caught me at the end of the parking lot, where two security men kneed me in the back and held my face to the pavement, bruising my neck.

When I was brought back, I was given a short-acting sedative and put down to rest for a couple of hours. After I woke up, Diane and Sandy, a nurse, informed me that to get better I have to start taking back control of my life. I am confused about how to take back control when they won't let me have any, but I do know that I will no longer ask for help. From now on I will keep to myself.

I think healthcare professionals should expect that mentally ill patients are unstable and should use discretion when making judgments or giving personal opinions. Mixed messages only cause patients more confusion about their treatment.

*August 11:* Today was the last case conference held with Dr. Black before he goes on vacation, leaving me in the care of Dr. Adams. I weighed in at

96.9 pounds, showing a loss of 3.5 pounds in a week. As a result, all privileges were taken away, I was confined to my room 24/7, and Eve was instructed to fill out my menus without input from me. I nearly snapped as I asked Dr. Black, "What do you want me to do?" to which he replied coldly, "Eat your way out of here." I lunged at him and said, "One day I will kill you." Making a threat for the future was the only power I felt I had over the situation. I was given the KOD and forced to sleep off my anger.

I woke up still angry, however. Both Karla and Daniel tried to converse with me, but I talked to no one. Silently, I made a decision that once I hit 100 pounds again I would quit smoking, since I realized they were using this addiction to control me and keep me working on the program.

*August 17:* Lance visited and gave me the gift of hope. He told me he was thinking about starting a support group for people suffering from anorexia nervosa and once I was well I could be a source of encouragement for others. He always manages to keep me looking to the future.

*August 19:* It's case conference day, and since I had already gained the required weight, I anticipated rewards. But Dr. Adams had a different approach to treatment. He said that if I ate everything for the next five days, I would be rewarded with smoking passes, but until then I would get no privileges. This upset me, and my emotional state had become so fragile that the slightest change could throw me into turmoil—which it did. The morning staff had made the mistake of leaving my shampoo in the room, and I squirted the security men with it each time they tried to enter. At one point, eight adults were scared off by shampoo, slipping and sliding around the room as they tried to catch me. When I eventually ran out of ammo, I was given another injection and left with only a blanket and mattress.

A little later, Leah stopped by, whereupon I pulled the blanket over my head, tired of being in a fishbowl for everyone to observe. When Leah said, "Sara, take the blanket off your face," I replied, "Whatever you tell me to do, I'm going to do the opposite." So Leah countered, "Sara, put the blanket over your face," and I answered, "Alrighty." We both burst into laughter. Then Leah said something that profoundly affected me: "Sara, I'm not mad at you, you're a good person, you're just going through bad times, which is bringing out bad behavior." From that day on, I did my best to live up to Leah's view of me, attempting to act like the woman I had the potential to be. It's amazing how much difference the right words can make.

*August 22:* I was given my art supplies the other day, so last night I went to work on a project for Leah's birthday, which is today. I began by making a big sign to hang on my door that read, "Happy birthday to my favorite natural blonde," referring to the many times Leah had teased me about my dark roots showing, as if I had been too busy to hit the salon lately. Previously, I had organized a little CNC surprise party and had my mother pick up a gift—a T-shirt from the club where I used to coach gymnastics, since Leah had said that when I recovered we would go to the adult class together for some fun, and I wanted to show Leah that I believed in my ability to recover. Finally, just before lunchtime, I prepared a chocolate cake—the "anorexic way," by cutting a photo of one out of a magazine and mounting it on cardboard. Leah was surprised and giggled as we spoke of eating her birthday cake for dessert. In doing all this, I realized that helping others feel good makes me feel good about myself—an insight I hope to use when I'm feeling down in times to come.

Later in the afternoon, Lance came to tell me that my father had returned home from work suffering from some kind of emotional breakdown, having acknowledged in his heart that he had in fact sexually abused me when I was a child. He made an appointment with a psychiatrist, a step in the right direction.

In my room, I now have a mattress, a bed frame, a nightstand in which to keep art supplies, and a table and chair. I arranged the furniture in a maze, calling it the "Rat Trap" to signify that no matter how I organize aspects of my life, reality remains the same—in particular, my time here. And the thing about my confinement in this maze is that the only way out is to nibble away like a small rat. The furniture expresses how I feel in this place, but my nurse said I should stick with my artwork instead.

So I wrote about my feelings, using illustrated nursery rhymes and fairy tales as metaphors. I landed in CNC because I was Jack Be Quick (escaped), but I got burned by the candlestick (caught). I feel like Mary, and everywhere I go my lamb (nurse) is sure to follow. I'm like little Jack Horner alone in my corner, feeling like Little Boy Blue. I'm like Jill, always trying to get some water. Poor Little Red Riding Hood (Eve), coming to bring food to Grandma but finding instead the big bad wolf (me). I feel like Goldilocks trying to fit into Baby Bear's bed (distorted body image). I fear I may end up like Pooh, eating so much I get stuck.

The story that most resembles my feelings is that of Hansel and Gretel: I am sent away by my family (staff) since they no longer want me around. The gingerbread house illusion is the hospital, which seems like a wonderful place for treatment but is too good to be true. I feel like Hansel in his cage, eating until I am plump enough to be "fed" to society. The stove represents three things: my fear of dying in the "fire" of life before I'm completely recovered, my hope that the staff's "fire" to help me does not burn out, and my smoking. The stones are showing the way back home, each characterizing an "issue" I must face. My home is just starting to be built.

*August 24:* I am relieved that I made it through the last five days, which was necessary to be granted four ten-minute smoking breaks per day. Dr. Adams increased my calories and wants me to eat my "phobic" junk foods. I seem to have lost my identity and am no longer Sara but Miss Anorexia Nervosa. Dr. Adams didn't offer much encouragement, saying, "You are so ill that I wouldn't be surprised if you are still here next summer. Come October, I think Dr. Black should renew your involuntary status for another three months." His remarks made me think that I need a lawyer, not a psychiatrist.

*August 30:* I had a spot weigh-in today. For another five days of eating, I will be rewarded with an extra two cigarette breaks per day. I believe this system is a better method of treatment, since it focuses on the consequences of my actions rather than a number on the scale. Dr. Adams informed me that Dr. Black is coming back from vacation next week. Chances are he isn't going to be pleased with my weight since I have gained only .6 pounds during his absence. I'd better deal with his reaction when it comes rather than dwelling on future problems now. Worrying about what tomorrow may bring is a terrible waste of time and energy since we can only know the present.

*September 1:* Dr. Black is back; it's case conference day; and I've lost .9 pounds. Since I spent the last two and a half months exercising between eight and eleven hours a day, my body has given up on me. I'm so exhausted that I stayed in bed for hours today trying to figure out where I might receive *real* treatment. CNC was a safety net in the beginning, but the current "motivational" therapy is sheer punishment.

*September 8:* Five days ago, a family meeting was called. My mother had asked to speak with Dr. Black, but when she, Lance, and Jackie arrived they were greeted instead by the entire staff, which caused Mom to feel ambushed. She told me that she looked at Jackie and muttered under her breath, "Okay, if we run into confrontation, we'll just put up the white flag and come back with an advocate." But the meeting went well, with both parties agreeing that while I was not ready for discharge, CNC was not working. It was decided that on September 8 I would be let out and placed back into the "population." In the meantime I would be granted four passes out of the hospital with my family, nights that I thoroughly enjoyed.

Each evening as I left the hospital, I felt like an alien experiencing earth for the first time. It was scary to be out in the world after three months of solitude, but at the same time it had never seemed more beautiful. I was in awe of simple things such as the scent of freshly mowed grass and puddles left after a rainstorm. I wished that everyone in the world could see through my eyes and feel so inspired by life's little miracles.

Today I was released from CNC. My new program, called "Sara's Care Plan," is one I have written and can commit to. I was returned to my private room and given the freedom to come and go, choose my own meals, eat alone, visit family and friends when I wish, and take walks with the staff. I also agreed to prepare my own meals and eat in public places with Karla—privileges that just might become tough pills to swallow.

## CHAPTER NINE

# A Taste of Freedom

$\mathcal{D}$*ay 39:* I have decided to once again incorporate exercise into my daily routine. Because of my addictive personality, I have to consciously set limits, so I am thinking one hour of exercise six days a week is sufficient. For the first time in years, I am using freedom of choice to make healthy decisions in my life. And perhaps as a result, over the past five and a half weeks of reflecting on my history, I have felt closer to being healed than at any time during my last three years of treatment. Maybe everything we need to know in life is within us, and our biggest job is to tap into these inner resources. Receiving proper therapeutic treatment is also important, however, and no one should feel ashamed to seek help.

My first week out of CNC provoked sensations that must be comparable to those a caged bird experiences the first time she is permitted to spread her wings once again and soar deftly into the vast, open skies. Despite the anxiety that accompanied this feat, I was ecstatic, for I was free.

At the start, I took morning walks with Karla, filled out my own menus with Eve's guidance, and made a list of meals I would prepare on my own. While I still manipulated my caloric intake, I cut back my exercising to three hours a day, one after each meal.

Unexpectedly, childhood friends I had not conversed with in ten years reestablished contact with me, and I relished their support. Melissa's daughter Jocelyn, who was living in the United States, became my pen pal.

Shelly, a neighborhood family friend, took me out for coffee. Former coworkers and friends from the West Coast started calling again, and I also launched new friendships within the hospital.

The rest of my week was perfect. I went out on passes with Lance and Mom, visited Janice and Gretchen, took walks by the river, shopped for groceries, and even bought new clothes. For the first time, I could appreciate what my mother had once said: "Look at the bright side of gaining weight, Sara—you get a whole new wardrobe."

Deciding to investigate what 100 pounds means to me, I reflected on my life before reaching that weight in comparison with my life afterward, and discovered a major contrast between the two periods. As a child, I had no control over the perverse touching and probing that was forced upon my body. Saying "No!" didn't stop my father from stroking my genitalia; nor did shoving my bed against the door protect me from his intrusions. Fortunately I was never aroused by the degrading and sexually violent episodes I endured, including the times I was forced to handle his penis or perform oral sex. Most likely this lack of response was rooted in the fact that the shameful exploits between my father and me were kept a secret, causing me to dissociate from the events.

Whereas during my childhood I lacked control over my actions, in adulthood I gained control but used it to violate my body. When I wanted to say no, I consented to multiple forms of mistreatment. For example, I was promiscuous; all the while, I allowed men to call me derogatory names in bed and I was aroused by sexual deviance. In addition to being a self-abuser, I lashed out violently at others, both physically and verbally, mostly because I didn't understand the extreme and contradictory perceptions going on inside my head. When I couldn't dissociate, I turned to drugs and alcohol. In effect, as a child I was a victim, while as an adult I had free will but made unfortunate choices.

*September 15, 1998:* At my case conference today, I weighed in at 94 pounds, having lost 2.5 pounds. Nothing was altered in my program, but Dr. Black said if I manipulated my meals there would be big changes. Eve asked me what my plan would be if I started living on the outside. The problem is I don't have one, and that's what is going to kill me. Sadly, after almost eight months of treatment my biggest concern remains my weight.

*September 17:* I made it through an entire day without manipulating my meals, but tomorrow will be different since I'm already thinking of ways to sabotage my food intake. I can't seem to resist manipulation, which starts with one little thing then gets completely out of hand. It's also true that I eat out of fear rather than for well-being.

*September 19:* I went with Lance to a jazz festival downtown, having received a pass for motivation "so I can see what I'm missing." But I came back early, still depressed over my illness. I am discouraged, as there is no difference between my condition now and last year. If anything, my fears of food and weight have intensified and I have lost all desire to fight them. It doesn't matter where I am living, at home or in the hospital, because with anorexia I miss out on everything anyway.

*September 28:* It's not that I want to give up on getting better, I just feel defeated by my negative mind. I can't stand the emotions that come with eating—guilt, shame, self-hate, feeling dirty—because they remind me of how I feel about my sexual abuse. And eating only what I am emotionally comfortable with is not an option, for there will never be enough to sustain me. If I go downhill, I will have to leave town, since I can't allow my family to watch me die or have anyone intervene again. So it is settled: if I become voluntary on October 16, when my status once again comes up for evaluation, I will leave not only the hospital but the town as well. My plan had little chance of succeeding, however, because I foolishly relayed the details to several nurses.

*September 29:* On this case conference day, I weighed 90.3 pounds. Eve increased my calories, but I told her it's pointless and a waste of food since I will not eat it. Dr. Black has called an eating disorders specialist from another city to come meet with me, talk to my family, give him a third opinion, and present a seminar to the staff.

*October 1:* This morning I had a phone conversation with my father, who sounded preoccupied and upset. He apologized and wanted me to help him remember what he did to me. He said that when I was young he suffered from depression and blocked out memories associated with those dark and difficult years. At least he admitted that he knows he did disturbing things to me and is unsure only of the particulars and the extent of the abuse.

Dr. Black won't allow us to meet, primarily because of my current instability, though he did say a supervised meeting could be arranged in the future. I assume Dr. Black is concerned about my father's volatility and believes that in time I will be better prepared to cope with another encounter. He also ordered me to keep the door to my room open.

In response to this increased control, I am refusing to be weighed and have started exercising in the open. I feel devoid of emotion and oblivious to anything outside my need for tight perimeters of self-control and defiance. Despite obvious dissatisfaction in the nurses' voices, I feel no remorse for having broken my commitment to them.

*October 2:* Karla brought me a book on sexual abuse today, but I told her I didn't want it. I have spent the last eight and a half months living in the past, and I just want to pretend the abuse never happened. Repressing the memories, I suspect, may cause them to haunt me later, but that's a chance I'm willing to take.

Things are getting precarious. Tina caught me manipulating my dinner, and I told her I just don't care anymore. On the weekends when Karla is away, only Linda will take me for walks since the rest of the staff no longer trusts me. Dr. Black said he heard I was making plans to leave town and is therefore going to try to renew my involuntary status on October 16, most likely for a duration of ninety days. He assured me that if I leave in two weeks I will probably die, and maybe that is what's supposed to happen.

*October 5:* Some of the nurses believe I haven't been the same since my release from CNC and that my compulsion to exercise has increased. Certainly, I am isolating myself from the other patients and I have lost faith in the team. My mother says my spirit appears to be broken. It is true that I often catch myself pacing the floor and I no longer laugh, write affirmations, read to the patients, or feel a sense of purpose in life. I am getting sicker by the day and have entered the danger zone again. My blood work shows a decreased red blood cell count, which causes the all-too-familiar symptoms associated with anemia. Indeed, the lanugo hair has grown back, I can't sleep, my ears are ringing, my sense of taste is off, and my bowels are barely functioning.

*October 7:* This afternoon Karla fought with me about my pacing, a behavior she says originated after my release from CNC. I consider my frenetic gait an actual by-product of solitary confinement, an impulse to relentlessly fight off the demons that purge my existence. "When will it be enough?" Karla asked, and I replied, "When I'm dead." I don't think I am suicidal, though it's possible I am trying to bring on a cardiac arrest. Intent on unbalancing my electrolytes, I don't eat anything containing potassium or sodium. Delusional and paranoid, I feel as though Dr. Black is the devil and the nurses are his puppets; agreeing to follow this program is tantamount to making a deal with the devil. I don't even trust my family.

*October 14:* Five days ago, Dr. Black changed my program, hired sitters to stay with me 24/7, and injected me with the KOD. Although I have little energy for writing, I want to record the miracle that occurred today. I had a most unusual visit from a messenger of a higher source, perhaps a guardian angel here on earth. Her name is Sonya and she is in her twenties, strikingly beautiful, well educated, and very spiritual. Sonya, who works at the tanning salon I once frequented, said that she has been praying for me ever since she first saw me and that God told her to talk to me. She urged me not to give up hope, because I am very much a part of his plan and will one day do great things. Sonya's visit makes me want to recapture my faith and ask God to speak directly to me.

Although Sonya's words of encouragement linger in my heart, my body and soul were unable to sustain the inspiration. Within days, I was once again slipping into self-destructive behaviors.

*October 18:* My weekend went pretty well. As a result, though I still have a nurse with me during the daytime, the night sitters have been canceled. So I exercise inexorably from midnight till 8:00 a.m. except when the male attendant or night-shift nurse appear during their hourly night checks. Generally, I'm good at not being caught. It's one of the few successes I enjoy.

On Saturday, Tina and I carved a pumpkin my mother brought in, and at night I was allowed to go out with Lance to my favorite café and then to the mall to buy Halloween decorations for my room. I hung them today, along with a beautiful hand-painted, wooden wall ornament Linda made for the occasion. As soon as I finished, Angie, my advocate from the summer, came in, letting me know she will be representing me at the hearing. I apologized for being judgmental toward her in July and admitted it was my own thoughts that had caused me to feel hopeless. She explained that this time my family would be present at the hearing, along with Dr. Black and the other members of the team. The decision will be made by the chair of the board, an independent psychiatrist, and a person from society. It sounds scary, but it will also be a chance for my family and me to voice our concerns.

*October 20:* I was weighed today for the post-hearing case conference and logged in at 83 pounds, indicating I have lost 15 pounds in one and a half months. Fortunately, at the hearing the board made me involuntary until January 16. Staying means I will not die.

*October 23:* The eating disorders specialist came today. She introduced herself as Debbie, and we talked about a change in medication, eating more, and psychotherapy, but nothing miraculous. I am beginning to see how extremely ill I am. I'm often complimented on being strong willed; however, that's the very trait preventing me from getting better.

Debbie recommended an eating disorders program that sounds therapeutic but is currently filled to capacity. Another option would be an in-patient care program in the United States, but the government of New Brunswick, which through Medicare has fully covered my hospitalization thus far, is not willing to provide funding for it. My time with Debbie made me realize how quickly the exhilarating taste of independence I experienced upon being released from CNC has soured. No sooner did they let me out of the box than I became trapped within the walls of my own despair. Clearly, freedom is not bestowed from without but rather ignited from within.

---

### Sara's Revised Care Plan

✳ Bed rest in room. Supervised bathroom and shower privileges. No yoga. No exercise at all.

✳ Let staff do laundry.

✳ Continue 1:1 nursing observation 24 hours a day.·

✳ No smoking or other out-of-room privileges.

✳ Dangerous personal effects to be removed from room.

✳ May have TV and VCR to watch movies.

✳ Meals are to be chosen by dietitian and fully completed by patient as her obligation. If meals are consumed in entirety, patient may have an extra 125 mls. of Ensure up to 3 times a day with small amount of ice; same to be taken by straw (no spoon). May also have extra fluids ($H_2O$, juice, but no coffee) as requested to stay hydrated, with small amount of ice. Herbal tea 2 times a day.

✳ Ensure sent on tray is not extra; it is part of meal, and as such must be finished. Also, patient may drink 1 cup of coffee with breakfast, and may not exchange coffee on tray for one from cafeteria or get extra coffee.

✳ Weigh weekly.

Sara is responsible for adhering to set plan. If she chooses not to, alternate means of ensuring nutrition will be initiated, such as intravenous feedings via total parenteral nutrition (TPN) or partial parenteral nutrition (PPN) that cannot be pulled out.

Sara is responsible for telling visitors whether she chooses to see them or not.

---

*Figure 2*

*October 30:* The verdict was announced after lunch today. Dr. Black, Daniel, Karla, Eve, and the head nurse came together; handed me a revised care plan (see figure 2); and told me I was being put on bed rest, will have 24/7 supervision, and if I choose not to eat will be placed on intravenous feeding. Just contemplating the obliteration of personal control these measures enforced, I doubted I would ever be sane again and concluded that my only alternative would be death. Wailing, I told them they had just put the last nail in my coffin.

## CHAPTER TEN

# SURVIVOR RESOLVE

*Day 47:* It's hard to believe that two years ago I was contemplating suicide, a victim's solution. Now I realize that I have one chance to be on this earth as Sara, and I don't intend to waste it anymore. For the first time since my discharge from the hospital, I had a meeting with my current psychiatrist and physiologist, Dr. Thirlwall and Tracy. They work out of a hospital two hours away, but it was worth the trip just to hear Tracy say, "Sara, now you're talking like a survivor."

The return to my hospital room at the end of October 1998 became a heavily medicated affair. In addition to injections, I was forced to take medication orally. My vision often hazed over, and my speech slurred. Mom talked to Leah, who agreed I was being overmedicated and convinced Dr. Adams to decrease the drugs. Both times Dr. Black went on vacation, he had me solidly medicated and I followed his program like a cow going to pasture. But I promised myself that after leaving this place I would strive to abide by my heart, not prescriptions scribbled by a doctor thinking more about his bloody vacations than my blood levels.

Each day, a different staff member sat at my bedside in an otherwise vacant chair I was still not permitted to occupy, confined, as I was, to bed rest. We did everything from playing I Spy to making origami and occasionally watching TV. After seeing the Martha Stewart show, one of the nurses rearranged my clothes, and I, being a perfectionist, thoroughly enjoyed the new organization of my wardrobe.

From midnight until 8:00 a.m. I had sitters, one of whom was a generous and compassionate woman with strong religious convictions who read to me from the Bible. She said that God had come to her in her prayers and told her he had plans for me, and that her church recited weekly prayers for my recovery, making me wonder how many guardian angels one person can have. While organized religion does not interest me, parts of the Bible do bring me closer to a higher being, so I was willing to listen. And soon I was sure I could hear God's message.

*November 24, 1998:* On this case conference day my weight was up. Dr. Black, having returned from his vacation, is increasing my antipsychotic drugs, hoping I will benefit from their tranquilizing effect. I hate this medication, because it disrupts my natural body signals, making me feel false hunger. The other change in my program consists of decreased observation: now I only have to be watched during each meal, as well as an hour before and after it.

*November 28:* It is excruciating to eat while being watched. Given my distorted body-image, I am embarrassed to put food in my mouth; it is a shameful and gluttonous task that shouldn't be witnessed by others. To make matters worse, I have been required to consume more substantial portions. Mortified, I eat with a colossal eye on me at all times. Not only have I lost the one thing I could control, but perched across from me is a Cyclops who seems to revel in my agony. I wonder if I will ever be able to enjoy eating in the presence of others.

As for the bed rest, on the other hand, it is the best treatment I could be receiving. The energy wasted while I compulsively exercised is now available for other activities. And while I no longer have therapy with Daniel, I occasionally work on my issues alone or escape into self-help books and television shows. Talk shows, especially, allow me to observe others in circumstances far more horrific than mine. I am encouraged to move forward by hosts such as Rosie O'Donnell, who suffers from an anxiety disorder, and Oprah Winfrey, a survivor of sexual abuse. While both these women appear to be struggling with issues related to food and weight, they are successful despite their less-than-ideal physiques. Clearly, people are much more than their appearance and the particular demons they are exorcising.

When I am not immersed in books or television, I watch videos. A few days ago, Dr. Black lent me his son's snowboarding videos, thinking they would offer me something to look forward to after my release. While riveted to the scenes of people surfing deftly downhill, I began to see an analogy between snowboarding and life: you plant your feet firmly on your board, try to stay balanced, and be grateful for the joy of the ride. Whether you choose to challenge the mountain or go with the flow, you recognize that your happiness is an outcome not of the expensive equipment involved but of the ride itself. You understand that danger exists—other people, trees, unexpected bumps, and other obstacles—but you find a way around them and try not to crash. With every turn on the mountain, you make new discoveries, including some about snowboarders. They come in all shapes, sizes, and skill levels, and have unique experiences on the mountain together. Alas, their time on the mountain eventually ends, as does everything in life, but they look forward to the prospect of more mountains to conquer.

*December 1:* At my case conference, I had gained another pound. Dr. Black again increased my calories by adding snacks. I was awarded two thirty-minute breaks with my family and am allowed to sit in my chair and go to TAG (Therapeutic Activities Group), but only if I eat the snacks (see figure 3).

I've decided to give up trying to control everything around me; rather than rock the boat, I will just allow the current to carry me along. This decision is based in part on my desire to get out of here and in large measure on a sense of feeling connected to God and his plan for my recovery. I believe that my life has been spared and I have been given the strength to prevail so that one day I might help others who are tormented by afflictions similar to mine. This change of heart has sparked within me an inner peace—something no one can take away as long as I stay positive. If I can get through this hell, I ought to be able to face anything life presents.

---

### Care Plan Revisions (12/1/98)

Sara's Care Plan remains in effect, with the following changes:

❋ Add 3 snacks per day—at 10:00 a.m., 2:30 p.m., and bedtime.

❋ Reduce 1:1 nursing observation from 24 hours a day to meal and snack times. One-hour supervision will be required after meals as well, but not after snacks. (Patient to use bathroom before eating.)

❋ If patient eats all meals and all snacks, the following privileges apply; otherwise, no privileges apply.

1. Patient may sit in chair.

2. Patient may go to TAG accompanied by a nurse or staff member.

3. Patient receives 2 half-hour passes per week to go to gift shop with family on Thursdays and one weekend day.

---

*Figure 3*

*December 5:* It is a sign of weakness to allow a man I don't trust—namely, Dr. Black—to control my body. Oddly, I can hold this thought and also regard it as a distorted way of thinking that I must change in order be happy in this world. I'm convinced that the more I cooperate with the program here, the better I will be, and, perhaps, the less defeated I will feel.

I am practicing a technique Daniel taught me a long time ago—how to turn shoulds and shouldn'ts into wants. For example, if the team says I "should" eat, my negative mind says I "shouldn't"; but choosing wellness, I can decide I "want to" get better. The more I transform shoulds and shouldn'ts, the easier it is to upgrade my outlook on life and feel peaceful inside.

*December 8:* At my case conference, I weighed 92.2 pounds, a gain of 1.4 pounds. My new privilege is to make chicken fajitas for two—and happily, Karla will be joining me for lunch. I'm still not allowed to smoke, but maybe I'm better off since it's a bad habit. What has happened to Sara the pessimist?

Dr. Black indicated that he will not be renewing my involuntary status, which means I'll be blowing this Popsicle stand on January 15, hallelujah! With that thought in mind, when I was allowed out of bed for thirty minutes this evening, I went outside to look at the stars. While gazing at the heavens, I was struck by the vastness of the grand scheme of things, how my illness and hospital stay amount to the tiniest fraction of my life's constellation, and that endless possibilities await me. From now on, when my universe seems constricted I will step outside at night and remember all the immense new galaxies there are to explore.

*December 10:* Everyone has commented on my new positive attitude. They aren't fully buying it, which doesn't matter since what counts is the belief I have in myself. The same holds true for self-esteem: in the end, all that should matter is what you believe in your heart. A hundred people can tell me I'm slim, smart, and beautiful, but if I feel overweight, uneducated, and ugly, these become the thoughts that guide my behavior. With low self-esteem, I exude negativity and lack of confidence; hide my beauty behind poor posture and too much makeup; cover my figure with oversized clothes; and meet with obstruction at work and in my relationships. I realize increasingly that my experience of life correlates directly with my attitude, and it's time to start having a good one.

*December 21:* I told Dr. Black that some "live wire" inside me is causing me to feel anxious, restless, and temperamental. His response was to put me on yet another medication. When I asked for information about the new pills, my request was ignored.

I am annoyed by my bulging belly, but apparently a distended stomach is normal with added pounds and in time the weight will distribute itself more evenly. Because my body feels worse, I object when people tell me I look better. It's odd, but to an anorexic "better" is interpreted as "fatter." I should write a book entitled *Things Never to Say to an Anorexic.*

By contrast, two of my high school friends gave me a snowboarding magazine for Christmas and a card that was priceless for an anorexic expected to gain weight. On the front were heads of lettuce with an X through them, and the message inside read, "Lettuce no, lettuce no, lettuce no."

*December 24:* It's Christmas Eve, and I am fully prepared for the holiday. Since December 1, Mom has been bringing me a decoration every night. And this past week I had her purchase handcrafted angel decorations for the nurses and gingerbread man ornaments for Dr. Black and the male attendants.

At my case conference two days ago, I had gained 2.6 pounds, so my privileges were increased (see figure 4). As a result, I was allowed to attend a Christmas play that Lance directed and dedicated to me, and in the morning go out to a bagel shop with Karla. The best reward I received is a pass to attend Jackie's Christmas dinner with my family.

*December 26:* Yesterday, Santa paid me two visits—one at the hospital and another at Jackie's house. Before I left for Jackie's, Mom had come to put my hair in two French braids with red ribbons, as she often lovingly did when I was a child. In fact, I usually wear my hair in two small pigtails as a comforting reminder. I enjoyed being with Lance, Mom, my nephew Tanner, Jackie, and her husband's family, but the buffet-style dinner was terrifying. When meals are sent to me, I'm used to completing them, like a robot, so I didn't know what an average portion would look like; my mother told me I did well considering the circumstances. Years ago, eating was like breathing—something I did without a second thought—but now I'm more scared of mashed potatoes than of jumping out of a plane.

*December 29:* At my case conference, I had lost .6 pounds. I played by the rules, but sometimes my body regulates on its own cycle, not Dr. Black's. He increased my calories and wants me to continue gaining until I leave. He does not think I'll be ready to go home on January 15, claiming I'd be setting myself up for failure. Since I will soon become a voluntary patient, the date of departure is my choice. As always, Lance had words of wisdom: "Just because someone throws you the ball doesn't mean you have to catch it." But alas, against all odds I have decided to leave, because I want to see the world again.

Now that I'm getting ready to live in the outside world, it is becoming apparent that my experiences with sexual abuse and mental illness have provided me with exceptional knowledge for adhering to God's plan for me. Toward that end, I have made a few decisions:

※ I will keep some of the pain alive within me as a constant reminder of my struggles, triumphs, and profound lessons from adversity.

※ I will work toward eliminating the stigma associated with sexually abused children and mental health patients.

※ I will advocate for the rights of women in the mental health system, and ensure that they are able to make informed decisions about their treatment and their lives.

---

### Care Plan Revisions (12/24/98)

With the exception of the following, patient is to continue with bed rest, supervision in shower, no yoga, and no exercising:

※ Patient may receive 2 smoking passes per day, for 5 minutes each, to be used during observation time after breakfast and dinner, and 5 minutes after p.m. snack (unobserved).

※ Patient may go out, accompanied by her occupational therapist, for morning snack today.

※ Patient may have pass to go, accompanied, to brother's play this evening.

※ Patient may have a 6-hour pass tomorrow, from 3:00 p.m. to 9:00 p.m., to spend Christmas with family. The patient must first complete her afternoon snack before departing; eat a buffet meal while out; and return in time to complete her p.m. snack.

※ Patient may have hair done, accompanied, one day next week.

---

*Figure 4*

✳ I will use the knowledge I have gleaned from the misfortunes of my treatment to help mental health professionals do their jobs with greater empathy and respect for the dignity of their patients.

In short, I hope to utilize in a good way everything I once viewed as bad, and in the process cultivate forgiveness and inner peace. I trust that when the time is right I will learn what I need to know, listen to my intuition, and allow my spirit to guide me.

Sometimes the most valuable transformations evolve from traumatic events and personal suffering. Certainly, although I have lived a far-from-perfect life, without the bad I might have missed out on the good. I will soon be better and able to use this experiential knowledge as a springboard to freedom from my past by building a more productive future.

*January 4, 1999:* Despite my reflections on living in the outside world, I haven't done much practical preparation. With eleven days left, I am still not selecting meals, going out alone, or developing social skills. It would be ideal if I stayed to learn survival skills, but I can't stand being here one more day. So it's time to sink or swim. I will work hard at furthering my recovery and hope for the best.

---

**Care Plan Revisions (1/5/99)**

Prior care plan remains in effect, with these changes:

✳ Patient may bathe and shower unobserved.

✳ Patient requires no observation during or after meals.

✳ Patient may choose meals, with dietitian's assistance.

✳ Patient may smoke as often as desired.

✳ Patient may have 2 meals out with her mother next week.

---

*Figure 5*

*January 6:* At my case conference yesterday, I weighed in at 100.6 pounds and am now free to do as I please. I am off bed rest; I don't have to be observed while eating; and I can bathe alone. I also have two passes to go out for meals with my mother, a challenge I'm up for. (See figure 5.)

Today, my first day off bed rest, I started manipulating my caloric intake again, convinced I had not earned the food. I rationalized these actions by telling myself that I was cutting back only until my metabolism is up to speed. Actually, these two months of bed rest have not only negatively influenced my bodily functions but wasted away my muscle tone and lowered my energy levels.

The moment I caught myself cutting back on my intake, I should have known I was not ready to leave. This reality struck home moments later, as I began planning ways to lose 5 pounds once I arrived home—like an alcoholic mentally arranging for just one drink on completion of her recovery program. As with alcoholism, when you suffer from anorexia you believe you are in control but actually you are controlled by the illness. Fortunately, at this point I did want to live, but I had to let go of the illness. Lance always believed I could overcome anorexia if I could just find my passion for life. The problem is you can't learn passion through therapy; it has to come from inside.

*January 7:* Dr. Black put fear into me today, saying that if I lose any weight he will be forced to renew my involuntary status. To ensure that I either maintain or gain, I am putting myself back on bed rest. My will to leave is stronger than my desire not to eat. Nine days of eating and not moving around is nothing compared to the past year I have endured here.

*January 10:* I went out for my first meal with my mother, but it did not go well. I wanted to eat at a restaurant where I was already familiar with the menu—another attempt to control my food intake, which angered my mother. She doesn't believe I am making sufficient effort to get better and, afraid I might leave prematurely, wants me to stay in the hospital for another month.

Sometimes I myself doubt that I am ready to leave. Tina asked me tonight what my plan was for life on the outside, and I had no answer. Her concern, on the heels of my mother's, made me realize that I was not the only one suffering from my illness. And whereas I once believed it would be better for my loved ones if I were dead, I now saw that while death might end the torture for me it would only prolong it for those who care about me. I must start thinking more about what I'm putting them through.

*January 12:* Dr. Black and I made arrangements for my departure. I am to see him and Dr. Maguire once a week and attend day therapy. My mother is setting me up with a private counselor named Joan, while Dr. Black is trying to get me a medical card so the medications will be more affordable.

*January 14:* With only two days left in the hospital, I anticipate my freedom with joy and yet I am scared, since no one believes I can survive on the outside. It is discouraging that I have failed in everyone's eyes before even trying, but I can't let negative thoughts bog me down. My challenge is clear: I need to prove that I can eventually beat this illness yet also consider whether there is any truth to their disheartening thoughts.

*January 15:* My last day has finally arrived, ten days short of a year. The next time I write in my journal, I will be out in the world.

## CHAPTER ELEVEN

# Out in the World...Briefly

$\mathcal{D}$*ay 54:* I started working as a volunteer for my mother's friend Janice, selling her poetry at the local farmer's market, all the while hoping to overcome my social anxiety. Having first developed symptoms—primarily fears of being poorly judged and feelings of inadequacy—during my time in CNC, I have had some success suppressing them, though lately they have gotten the better of me.

Apart from working at the market each Saturday morning, I remain relatively isolated, though no longer a singular figure caged in a stark, windowless room. On the contrary, the setting here at my father's house is conducive to examining my lost childhood, the mental illnesses with which I've been diagnosed, and the combative and demeaning treatment methods I have undergone. In facing the truth of these aspects of my life, I am managing to unload personal baggage that has weighed me down for as long as I can remember. In the years to come, I don't want to be haunted by a tortuous past riddled with shame; and to ensure that's not my fate I sometimes shout to the world, from the safety of my father's basement: "This is who I was, and you can either accept or reject me. I'm now ready to live life to my fullest potential, saying good-bye to disgrace and indignity, and hello to paths not yet taken."

Reaching out to assist Janice, whether or not it's actually enhancing my social skills, is helping me maintain a state of well-being. I have begun giving my "anorexic clothes" to a charity—symbolic of my promise never to go back to destructive eating patterns. And my weight is on to stay; I do not plan to return to the agony of losing pounds only to be forced to gain them again. Also underscoring my commitment to change is the fact that I have had my hair cut short, letting go of my pigtails and accepting the fact that I am an adult.

Despite my intention of becoming well when I left the hospital in mid-January 1999 after a full year of institutionalization, I lacked the self-control necessary to maintain a healthy state. It could be because I was discharged with insufficient coping mechanisms in place, or without transitional counseling or even an overnight pass—all of which are routine elements of a discharge plan. And while Dr. Black had made sure I left with a medical card, access to my prescribed medications could not compensate for the fact that I had left the hospital emotionally unfit, and physically, only marginally stable.

In any case, medication is not a means to an end, and within my first week out in the world I was starving myself with increased rigidity, even counting the 5.6 calories in a stick of gum. My obsession with personal hygiene had also spiked, and I was showering every hour. In addition, I did yoga daily, as well as aerobics and a toning routine with small weights. And I went for power walks around town, envisioning myself a woman on a mission.

As planned, I attended day therapy, but I merely went through the motions without absorbing anything of value. I also took a correspondence course in nutrition, half thinking it would enhance my education but ultimately using the information to further my obsession with food. In both arenas, I lied frequently and resorted to other manipulation strategies to maintain control.

*February 1, 1999:* I have been living at my mother's house and, since being discharged fifteen days ago, have lost almost 10 pounds. During my second weekly visit with Dr. Black, he noted my rapid weight loss, commenting on my protruding cheekbones. He also stated that while he wanted to give me the chance to regain control over my life, he now feared

I'd be unable to handle my illness alone. I, on the other hand, regard myself as a gymnast solely responsible for her performance but requiring coaching along the way.

*February 3:* I started seeing Joan, the private counselor, but sessions are a waste of money because I'm still unwilling to be part of a team. The gymnast in me is quite sure that people in recovery from an eating disorder, while well advised to ask professionals for information and support, must ultimately help themselves. Even so, it's good to know there's a therapeutic environment in the vicinity, as the outside world is proving to be much more overwhelming than I originally anticipated.

*February 12:* After settling into my mother's house, I contacted Gretchen and began working out at a gym in a nearby recreation center one or two days a week under her supervision. Thinking I might enjoy breaking out of my isolation and boredom by also volunteering at the recreation center, she set up an interview for me with the director, Melodie, a former patient of Dr. Black's, who personally knew a great deal about eating disorders. She gave me a respectable position and made me feel competent and useful. But I was to discover that a recreation center is a bad place for an obsessive anorexic to work, for I was soon exercising both before and after my work shifts—a routine I seem unable to disrupt. Although I know excessive exercise is self-destructive, I cannot silence the taunting voice in my head that commands me to do it and, simultaneously, engage in minimal food consumption. Like many other people who are mentally ill, I am aware that my thinking is irrational; however, I remain too powerless to rectify the inner directives that prevent me from achieving a state of well-being.

Although I did not initially inform Dr. Black of my new exercising rituals, during our third encounter he surmised that I must be taking drastic measures to achieve such rapid weight loss. At that point I told him about my routine, but he did not suggest that I quit my volunteer position. While he clearly feared for my future, he must have considered it important for me to engage in activities that restore self-esteem.

*February 26:* Having been segregated from the outside world for so long, I lack the self-assurance and social aptitude needed to seek friendships, so I have gone back to isolating myself by not answering the telephone. From time to time, Shelly takes me to a movie, but my self-starvation keeps me from focusing on the plot or even carrying on a simple conversation afterward. It's as if the majority of nutrients I consume go toward sustaining vital bodily functions and the rest are expended on obsessive thoughts of food, weight, and exercise.

Curiously, my inability to converse does not stop people from telling me about messages they receive about God's plan for me. Every few days I am privy to one such testimonial or another, yet I continually wonder whether they are true or just reflective of people's concern because I look so ill. Before my illness, I considered myself an atheist and a "sinner" for not being a Christian, and could not fathom God speaking to anyone about me. During and after my hospitalization, however, I have occasionally felt the presence of a higher source within me, delivering an infusion of peace and hope.

*March 14:* Of all my character traits, perhaps the worst is my impulsiveness. During a snowstorm four days ago, after heading home from the recreation center, I suddenly felt tired, hungry, and unwilling to face another day. Upon entering my mother's house, I packed a small suitcase, taking only my famous green Snugabyes and medication. I left a message on my mother's answering machine stating that I was going away for a few days to allow her some time alone. Then I went to a liquor store for rum and to my usual pharmacy, telling the pharmacist I was going out of town for a few weeks and that Dr. Black had said it would be all right to fill my prescriptions early. Amazingly, he asked no questions, made no phone calls, and proceeded to fill my prescriptions—something no pharmacist would ordinarily do without a doctor's authorization, especially when the medications involve antipsychotics, antidepressants, tranquilizers, and sleeping pills. Then, as before, I took a cash advance on my credit card and checked into a local motel, prepared to end my life.

Meanwhile, a search for me had commenced in earnest: Janice had begun driving around in the blinding snowstorm; Lance and Jackie were calling motels; and my mother was on the phone with Dr. Black, who advised her to call my pharmacy and the police and have me brought to the hospital if located. I had just finished bingeing on a bottle of booze and was about to start on the pills when the police knocked on my door. I explained that I was giving my mother a vacation from me and getting a little R&R for myself. They agreed that I had not broken any laws, but insisted I go to the hospital to be checked. So I agreed, but when I arrived Dr. Black decided to detain me as long as he legally could, which was seventy-two hours. I did not take the news very well; and although he had security with him, I attacked him, kicking and punching harder with each strike he deflected. As a result, I was given the KOD, slept for seventy-two hours in CNC, then walked out of the facility.

It later became important to acknowledge that there was nothing anyone could have done to prevent my suicidal impulses from surfacing, including my family and friends. I have since spoken with many people who have tried to take their own lives, among them some who were later successful, and the driving factors in each instance are immense personal suffering, feelings of hopelessness about the future, and an inability to cope with the anguish. In the end, choosing life or death is up to each individual, and thus family and friends should not blame themselves for a loved one's suicide.

*March 30:* Soon after leaving the hospital, I underwent a major change: my will to starve was overridden by a desire to eat. I would starve all day and binge in the evening, passing the intake off as an effort to gain weight; then I would take laxatives and indulge in a full night of exercise. I did not realize at the time that I had traded one eating disorder for another, having now become bulimic. Bulimia nervosa is characterized by frequent binge eating followed by purging through vomiting or other methods. Like anorexics, bulimics have an extreme fear of weight gain and a preoccupation with food. Following a few weeks of engaging in bulimic behaviors, I could no longer handle the distress of feeling out of control, and once again I contemplated suicide. Perhaps subconsciously wishing she would intervene and save me from myself, I told Joan I'd decided that death was my only option. Although I did not have a plan in place, I knew it was only a matter of time before my desperation would result in action.

One night in early April, after eating three muffins and feeling completely numb, I walked into the house, passed my mother without saying a word, and prepared a bath, so I would be clean and pure for death. After bathing, I ingested all four bottles of my medication, put on warm pajamas with feet, and snuggled into bed. The last thing I recall before passing out was attempting to write a note.

Again I was rescued. While I had been bathing, my mother and Janice went out for coffee and, suspicious of my behavior, returned within an hour, at which point my mother attempted to wake me up. Only half conscious, I spoke with a slur and made no sense, whereupon my mother, by now aware of the drill, gathered the pill bottles so the doctor would know what I had swallowed, then drove me to the hospital. In the ER, there wasn't much they could do for me other than administer charcoal through a nasal gastric tube and monitor my vitals. My mother eventually went home and was later notified that I had developed pneumonia after aspirating vomit, had been placed in the intensive care unit (ICU), and was unresponsive. My chances of survival were not promising.

Because of the bright lights in the ICU, when I awoke I immediately thought I was in heaven—until I saw the tubes, heart monitor, oxygen mask, and catheter. At first, my motor skills were off and I was not fully coherent. There was nothing I could do but pray that since my life had been spared, the functioning of my brain would be, too.

Moments later, the reality of my situation had sunk in and I was terrified that I might not live. Seeking the comfort and reassurance of my mother, I asked a nurse to phone her. Much to my dismay, the nurse returned minutes with a disturbing message: "Your mother called earlier and informed the staff that she and your sister had decided to visit your grandmother in Moncton." Some part of me knew that my mother, hurt and angered by the turmoil I perpetually caused in their lives, was unwilling to surrender to my illness. But no matter how much I tried to sympathize with her anguish, I experienced her decision to leave town as a profound rejection. I had never felt more alone in this world.

I was soon moved to a medical floor and placed under constant supervision. But no sooner did my strength return than I had the urge to run. I remember saying to the nurse, "I'm sorry, but I have to go. I won't be returning to the psychiatric unit." Immediately a brigade of nurses entered the room, making me feel anxious and claustrophobic, so I took off like a bolt of lightning in my footed pajamas. Codes were called over the loudspeaker as I ran out the front entrance and into the nearby woods.

Realizing I was no match for the security guards who were fast on my heels, I surrendered, collapsing on the soft ground. Jeffery, a guard who is now Tina's husband, scooped me up and, cradling me in his arms, carried me out of the woods and into the hospital parking lot, where I could hear the other guards joking about my captivity. Crying on Jeffery's shoulder, I asked him to let me go. But Jeffery, who appeared not to take pleasure in my misery, said, "Sara, I am sorry. We've been given orders. You are to be taken directly to CNC."

Like a wild mustang dropping dead of fright after being captured, I slipped into a long, cold silence, defeated and dispirited. I had lasted only two and a half months in the outside world.

## CHAPTER TWELVE

# The Throes of Isolation

*Day 61:* Over the past nine months, I have been corresponding with a man I met on the Internet, and today I met him in person. He is the first man I have allowed to get to know me mentally and emotionally before physically. Although I don't see our relationship evolving beyond friendship, I now feel that when the time is right I will be able to pursue a healthy partnership—one characterized by mutual integrity and respect.

As the security guards brought me through the back doors of CNC and Linda injected me with the KOD, I sobbed repeatedly, "I couldn't survive in the outside world. I just wanted to die." In the same way that my mother knew the drill for my suicide attempts, I knew the protocol for solitary confinement: I slipped off my pajamas, put on the baby blue cotton hospital gown Linda handed me, and curled up on the mattress on the floor, crushed by my failed escapade yet relieved to be in familiar, predictable surroundings.

A week later I was moved into a semi-private room, but I hated sharing my space. It stopped me from exercising, since I was too embarrassed to work out in the company of a stranger. It prevented me from journaling, as I was sure my inner thoughts would be read by my curious roommate. Even sleeping was uncomfortable with someone so close by.

Despite my aversion to sharing the room, I admired my roommate—a wonderful woman who spent hours each day crocheting a blanket that I thought was for her grandchild but turned out to be for me. Although it is said that psychiatric patients often struggle to maintain their sanity, she and others on the ward were among the most compassionate, generous, and talented individuals I had ever encountered. In many ways, the people in my initially muted world were now becoming increasingly alive for me. And while they may have been haunted by demons, to me these individuals were not mental patients but rather good people who had mental problems, which made me think I might be a good person, too.

*April 15, 1999:* Being back on involuntary status in the hospital reminds me of an entry I recorded in my journal almost a year ago, which I entitled "Nightmare on Psych Street":

> *Despite the diversity of people here, we all have two things in common: fear of never overcoming our illness and, by association, fear of being discharged and then relapsing. Certainly, on days when you can no longer remember your life before becoming ill, you question whether recovery is a viable option.*
>
> *Today they are discharging a woman who is nervous about her ability to cope on the outside. While assuring her she would be fine, I spotted a newly returned patient—depositing a cherry on my sundae of doubt. Seven weeks ago, this patient had left glowing with happiness as we voted her "most likely to succeed"; yet here she was again, shaky and teary eyed, demonstrating how quickly and easily a woman with apparent control over her illness can slip. This nightmare challenges me to face my fears and anxieties, and make some decisions. For one thing, I plan never to return, because I intend to leave only when I am mentally, emotionally, and physically recovered. For another, I must keep reminding myself that a fear is only a thought in my mind, which I am free to either dismiss or adopt as a reality. And third, while I believe in my heart that I will never have to return, all I can really do is fight for wellness and hope for the best.*

Reviewing these thoughts as an involuntary patient is disheartening. Janice, noticing that am losing my spirit again, wrote a poem to help me recapture it. This woman, at age sixty-five, seems to understand me better than anyone, perhaps because she once had a near-death experience and ultimately found her purpose. We both realize deep down that we are destined for other things before our time on earth is finished.

*May 1:* After a thirty-day period back at the hospital, the question of my status came before the chair of the tribunal, who decided today to reinstate me as an involuntary patient. It is difficult to win against a psychiatrist who views you as a risk to yourself, especially if you've recently attempted to take your life. Actually, I can see the point: mandated treatment is not so much about undermining a person's self-determination as it is a means for saving a life that might otherwise be lost to self-destruction. So despite losing my fight for voluntary status, I'd have to say I'm lucky to live in a society that reaches out to those who hurt.

*May 17:* Last week, Dr. Black decided I should undergo electric convulsive therapy (ECT) to combat the acute depressive symptoms I have been exhibiting since my return to the hospital. ECT, commonly known as "shock therapy," I was told, isn't the violent, debilitating intervention Randall Patrick McMurphy received in the movie *One Flew Over the Cuckoo's Nest.* Rather, the patient is given a muscle relaxant and general anesthesia; the patient's brain is then stimulated through electrodes that have been placed on precise locations on the head, either unilaterally, which stimulates one side of the brain, or bilaterally, which stimulates both sides; and the stimulation causes a controlled seizure that lasts for about a minute and is thought to temporarily change the way the brain receives certain chemicals, such as serotonin and dopamine. The procedure is usually performed by a psychiatrist after other forms of treatment, such as medication or psychotherapy, have proven unsuccessful. Typically, in-hospital patients receive between six and twelve treatments, up to three per week, while some are given additional maintenance treatments, usually on an out-patient basis.

I consented to Dr. Black's recommendation for two reasons. The first was that I had exhausted my treatment options and regarded ECT as a last resort in my quest for inner peace. The second reason was rooted in a desperate need to believe that my doctor, despite his often objectionable treatment methods, knew what was best for me.

My first session was the scariest. When the anesthesiologist entered the room to apply the sedative, images of brain-dead McMurphy and his band of catatonic and hallucinating comrades on the "Disturbed Ward," danced through my head. My heart raced as they put me to sleep; I prayed I would wake up alert and coherent. Ten minutes later, as is customary, I regained consciousness. This "last ditch" form of therapy was repeated three days a week for one month, and the results were less than desirable. While for some patients the aftereffects of ECT involve sore muscles, nausea, headache, or partial memory loss, which is said to reverse in about six months, I experienced a short-term high after each treatment and, once the treatments had ceased, an extremely low phase, along with mental confusion and memory loss. To date, I can remember only fragments of events from this period of time.

*May 28:* I am no longer being forced to eat, but rather encouraged to continue eating three meals and three snacks a day. To challenge my fears, I asked Eve to send in all my phobic foods, including burgers, fries, and sweets, which I proceeded to devour. Suddenly I could eat these foods because, in addition to receiving ECT to stabilize my condition, I was also on high doses of antipsychotic medication, which increased my appetite. But rather than testing my fears, I was really bingeing on these foods to protect me from my feelings and to avoid social encounters. As with anorexia, bingeing is a way of punishing my body by bringing on physical pain and emotional numbness. I also suspect that looking sickly or being fat shields me from men. The most interesting reason I binge, however, is that I associate food with love and attention. When I eat, the team and my family are pleased with me and also, picking up where my mother as nurturer left off, I derive solace in times of sorrow.

Eventually, Dr. Black tried to end my bingeing by enforcing a rule against it. But I stood my ground against his control tactics by trading packs of cigarettes my mother had brought for food that another patient's mother had brought. As before, I was on an obsessive mission.

*June 20:* Earlier this week, I reached 130 pounds and they stopped weighing me. I had gained the last 20 pounds very quickly, one week looking frail and ill, and the next big and bloated.

This afternoon, a patient asked me, "Sara, why are you eating so much?" and I replied, "Because the day I step out of here is the day I die, and gaining weight is a way to seal the deal for death." Ironically, I interpreted anorexia (which was killing me) as a means for moving toward wellness, and binge eating, without actual purging through exercise, as admitting to defeat and effectively giving up.

But weight was not my only obsession. As a recent CNC evacuee, I was routinely placed on room arrest and allowed only occasional ten-minute breaks, circumstances that renewed my obsession with time. I carried around a small black digital alarm clock, scared that I would get in trouble for being so much as a minute late in returning from a break. I was less afraid of disciplinary action than I was about risking alienation from the staff, from whom I already felt dangerously isolated. I was not close to my nurses anymore, and Daniel and Karla never visited. I ached for the warmth of human connections, and fortunately I'd occasionally speak with Joyce, a social worker who at that point in my life was the next best thing to sliced bread.

*June 22:* Although I have achieved my target weight, it is evident to the staff and my family that pounds are no longer the issue. The underlying reality is that I have traded one form of eating disorder (anorexia) for another (binge eating), signifying that my illness has worsened. Indeed, the more my weight increases, the further I spiral into the hellhole of depression, decreasing my odds of recovery.

In response, Dr. Black has again attempted to place me in an eating disorders clinic, but as before, his efforts have been unsuccessful. Another option, proposed by Debbie, was to move me to a hospital where I could be under the care of a female psychiatrist, but the staff was unable to find a practicing female psychiatrist in my hometown. It was therefore decided that I should be relocated.

Until today, I could not imagine leaving my family, although I was mortified to think of them witnessing the hideous transformation I was undergoing with this rapid weight gain. I was less resistant to the idea of leaving the hospital, since my support network here had collapsed: I no longer trust the nurses, have only disdain for Dr. Black, and sense a marked breakdown in communication among my team. Then an event that occurred this afternoon unmistakably catalyzed my willingness to go: I overheard a nurse commenting inappropriately about my recent weight gain, and although the remark reflected her concern, it still hurt. The incident further alienated me from the staff, and it soon became evident to the team and my family that, lacking strong rapport with the staff, I would never voluntarily participate in any form of treatment.

*June 25:* After two thirty-day involuntary commitments and one nearly sixty-day period as an involuntary patient, I have been transferred to a new treatment facility, where I am to retain my involuntary status and work with a female psychiatrist. This facility is in Moncton, where my mother's parents live, two hours from my hometown.

My family was notified late last night, but I was not informed until ten minutes before my departure this morning. When Dr. Black gave me the news, I fell to the floor in tears, feeling stunned, abandoned, and unloved. Then everything happened in a blaze of motion, eliminating any possibility of good-bye to my family, which was not permitted, or even time to change out of my bathrobe and slippers. Within minutes, a woman from the sheriff's department had arrived to assist with the transport and began railing against psychiatric patients in general, and me in particular. Staff members who witnessed the events later wrote letters of complaint to her boss, but in the heat of the incident, unhinged by her derogatory remarks as I was about to step into the unknown, I trembled from head to toe, scared and confused.

Spectators lined the sidewalk as I was escorted out of the hospital by the offensive woman on one arm and a male member of the sheriff's department on the other. Feeling like a common criminal, I was ushered into a caged restraining area in the back of a blue sheriff van. As we pulled out of the hospital parking lot, I stared out the back window at the familiar landscape, tears streaming down my face.

For the duration of the trip, the two escorts conversed among themselves but never spoke to me. Occasionally I would turn and peer between the bars wondering if I was even present, and imagining that perhaps my life was unfolding without me. I had no way of gauging whether I was a mere spectator or active agent, and whether the transfer would help or further torment me. All I knew was that my entire world was about to change.

As the van pulled up to a light along the outskirts of Moncton, I began to doubt my ability to engage in treatment with new caregivers in an unfamiliar setting. For one thing, I had grown so accustomed to isolation I was terrified of human interaction and prayed that the patients at the new facility would steer clear of me out of fear. To ensure such an outcome, I told myself, I could always hide silently behind the heavily medicated and heart-numbing stare I had cultivated over the past month. A second problem was that while Dr. Black seemed to have faith in my recovery and the good sense to know when I could be better served by another psychiatrist, I still seethed with anger toward him and wondered whether I could ever trust another shrink. As for the abruptness of the transfer, I felt betrayed by my family for consenting to it and so deceived and hurt by my former team that I vowed never again to trust a group of healthcare professionals. Inwardly and outwardly, I had lost hope.

## CHAPTER THIRTEEN

# Finding Inner Security

*Day 68:* Stepping outside my father's house invariably means confronting the stigma of mental illness. Old acquaintances talk to me as if I were violent, dumb, weak, lazy, or suffering from some inherent character flaw. One woman routinely stops me on the sidewalk, asking, "So, dear, have you pulled yourself together yet?" Teenagers sometimes jeer at me or mutter "psycho" under their breath. Other people, perhaps fearful that psychiatric disorders are contagious, shun me entirely, putting an invisible wall between us. While on a pass from the hospital, I would almost always feel ostracized by these forms of discrimination, thinking they were sparked by intolerance; I now think the cause is ignorance, which can at least be remedied.

Curiously, while townspeople recoil from my illness, my father appears to embrace it. He talks to me as if I were a little girl, his words ringing with sincerity, regret, and raw sentiment. Some days he attempts to nurture my soul with delicious food from the local bakery. It is as if my dependence on him for food and shelter has prompted him to take back the role of father and caregiver. I see these reparenting efforts as something he is driven to do to fulfill his own needs, born out of shame and guilt. But rather than attempt to retrieve the mantle of the "good father," he would be better off acknowledging present realities: I am twenty-four, *never* to be his little daughter again, and disinclined to letting him escape his torturous past. Frankly, I'm more concerned with scaling the wall to wellness than helping him purge the demons that haunt his soul.

On my second postdischarge visit with Dr. Thirlwall, she told me I had the right to see my files, but I declined, since what matters is not people's judgments of me but rather how I view myself. Just as I will not let the townspeople's dire predictions or my father's infantilizing influence my ability to grow, neither will I allow mental health professionals to hold me back. I will live my life loud, not in the hushed tones of weakness and dependency that foster mental health stereotypes which tend to be as debilitating as the illnesses themselves. I will face down these prejudices and personally dictate the means for maintaining my mental health.

It was on a Friday that I arrived at my new place of treatment in Moncton, and since the weekend had begun, I was left nearly alone to explore my new environment. The surroundings emitted a positive energy that, combined with my reading of the *Adult Psychiatry Information Booklet,* which was awaiting me in my room, left me optimistic about the treatment I would soon receive. The booklet included the following details:

> *Remember, you are here for yourself, so keep focused on you and getting the help you need. During your admission and with your consent, the nurse will search your belongings for sharp objects such as razors and scissors and for medication. You will be present during the search. . . . During your stay, if you should act or talk about harming yourself the staff with your consent will search your room and belongings. . . . Each patient has their own needs and problems. Acceptance of all the differences and respect for each other help keep the unit a place in which to feel better. . . .*
>
> *You as a patient will be the central part of the patient care team. You will be asked to participate in the decision-making process. We encourage you to ask questions. . . . Let other members of the patient care team know about your feelings—they may not know. Ask for information about your illness and treatment options. . . . The team will provide such treatment as individual therapy, family counseling. . . . You may need a psychologist for an assessment, one on one and/or couple therapy, based on your needs. Using*

*questionnaires and other tests, psychologists evaluate your feel-*
*ings, thoughts, personality, memory, and mental ability . . . to*
*help with your diagnosis and treatment. In one-to-one therapy*
*you will work together toward understanding and treatment of*
*your problems. . . . A social worker . . . will discuss and help with*
*such things as your personal, family, and social situation. . . . It is*
*important to your treatment that you come to understand how*
*family relationships have been and are involved with your crisis*
*or illness and how this affects relationships between family mem-*
*bers. . . . Occupational therapists . . . assist people in becoming all*
*they can be, especially in the areas of self-care, productivity, and*
*leisure. . . . The dietitian provides weekly nutrition classes on the*
*unit. . . . The recreational program is available for all patients on*
*the unit. Its goals are to promote quality of life, self-esteem, social-*
*izing, and interaction through leisure activities. . . . The [mission*
*of the] Patient Advocate Services . . . is to inform patients of their*
*rights, to represent them at tribunal or review board hearings,*
*and to ensure that the Mental Health Act and rights of the patient*
*be respected at all times. . . .*

Smoking was permitted off the unit between 7:00 a.m. and 9:30
p.m. with written permission from a doctor. In the meantime, I could
smoke in CNC, which was much different from the CNC at the hospital, with its common area where patients were allowed to smoke
seven times a day, four rooms with cameras, and a nurses' station that
monitored the patients. Although at this new facility there were only
two private rooms, all the patients had space to themselves. Every
unit consisted of four small rooms, each with a bed, desk, closet, and
a curtain for privacy; a small central living area; a bathroom; and a
shower.

There were two free phones we could use between 7:00 a.m. and
midnight. We were also permitted to watch TV anytime during the day, as
long as it didn't interfere with therapy. Nights were strictly for relaxation—
usually we all gathered to watch a movie and socialize in the main common area of the ward, where we could stay until midnight during the week

and 1:00 a.m. on weekends. Altogether there were two common areas offering access to two TVs, a VCR, a pool table, a washer and dryer, a stereo, and a hair salon.

Along with permission to smoke, patients could earn cafeteria privileges, walking rights, and night and weekend passes. And although we had to wear street clothes during waking hours, Dr. Thirlwall knew I had no clothes that fit and had been living in pajamas for a year and a half; she therefore allowed me to wear hospital gowns for the first month, which was fine with me since it helped me remain oblivious to my new size. Overall, I was comfortable with the arrangements.

Even so, my first weekday was extremely difficult. The nurse taking my vitals said I weighed 167 pounds, which caused me great dismay, heightened by indignation over the fact that Dr. Black had not allowed me to be weighed after reaching 130 pounds. But ironically, knowing my weight only made me want to binge more because of my feelings of shame.

*July 7, 1999:* When I first met Dr. Thirlwall, my intuition told me she was the right psychiatrist for me. Stern yet fair, she appreciated my sense of humor, listened to me as if every word mattered, and placed no restrictions on my eating. Her main concern was that I work on my "issues" with a psychologist every day, and she decreased my antipsychotic medication to help me take part in these sessions actively and in a coherent manner.

Aware of my weight concerns, Dr. Thirlwall allowed me to meet daily with a dietitian, who helped me fill out menus. She also had the pharmacist talk to me about the possible effect of high doses of antipsychotic medication on sharp weight gain. It turns out that while the meds may have increased my appetite, contrary to my earlier belief they did not contribute to my binge eating. Dr. Thirlwall's invitations to me to participate in my treatment let me know that my life will soon be different.

*July 26:* Earlier this month I met a twenty-eight-year-old woman named Julie, and we became fast friends. We had a similar history and understood each other very well. Every two days, we made or bought a little gift or card to show our fondness for each other. We laughed, hugged, cried, and even did private counseling with a psychologist together once a week. On weekends when Julie was granted a pass to leave, we would both feel sad that she had to go home to an alcoholic husband. Julie, I soon learned, loved marijuana, and we began smoking weed together outdoors every day while on cigarette breaks.

Nor were Julie and I the exception. Many patients here get high, some to numb their grief and others, like myself, to enhance a feeling of acceptance and bonding. Often shunned by family, friends, and community, psychiatric patients can form especially close-knit relationships.

During the months I spent getting high, I was caught only once. After a nurse observed Julie and me watching a video of Pink Floyd, munching on junk food, and laughing hysterically, we were given a urine test. Afterward, Julie was reprimanded harshly and told she would be immediately discharged the next time she got high, while I, surprisingly, was merely encouraged to use better judgment. I believe Dr. Thirlwall refrained from disciplining me because I was a relatively new and vulnerable patient to whom she wanted to send some important messages:

"You are accepted unconditionally here."

"We trust you to use better judgment."

"Healing comes from the inside out, and you have the inner strength to find healthier ways."

"Don't rely too heavily on others to make you well. Trust yourself."

"We believe in you, and now you must, as well."

Implicitly, Dr. Thirlwall had given me an infusion of hope and promise for better days, all the while laying the foundation for a stronger me. As a result of not being unduly penalized for making bad choices, I began to trust that honesty would help me recover.

I fully understood the need for logical consequences too, provided that they were timely. At the hospital, however, they were delayed and therefore maddening and counterproductive. Because team meetings and weigh-ins took place each Tuesday, that's when Dr. Black would announce consequences for misconduct that had occurred anytime during the previous week. And if I manipulated my intake on a Wednesday or broke a rule on Thursday, and was not punished until the following Tuesday, bombs would explode inside me upon hearing the news; by then, the correlation between his announcement and my actions had invariably become lost in the haze of time, which offered me no incentive for behavioral change.

*July 28:* A significant development for me has been the opportunity to interact with two nurturing male nurses, Pat and Dale, both of whom are gentle and kind. Pat often sits at my bedside as I weep uncontrollably about my apparently incurable illness, reassuring me that brighter days will follow, whereas Dale accompanies me on daily walks so I won't feel alone or overwhelmed.

I have also come to love nearly all the male attendants. Big Tony is like a giant teddy bear. Richard loves sunflowers probably as much as I do and says they reflect potential. Herc is sarcastic and funny. And Rowland, highly intelligent, is a great conversationalist.

*July 30:* Once again, change threw my life into turmoil when Dr. Thirlwall took a much-deserved vacation, leaving me under the care of Dr. Alexander, whose personality clashes with mine. He altered my program too fast, abruptly decreasing my antipsychotic medication, stopping my sleeping medication, giving me a different room, and making me wear street clothes. (I squeezed into my old T-shirts and tights for a few days until my mother was able to bring in new clothes, at which point I was forced to reconcile two self-images: the anorexic size 0 new patient with the overweight size 13 veteran patient.) The hardest change to accept was Dr. Alexander's decision to prohibit my interactions with Julie, believing it was not a healthy relationship—an insight I later realized was true.

*August 13:* Unfortunately, Dr. Alexander was present yesterday for my second review board hearing, along with an independent psychiatrist who was concerned about my ongoing hospitalization as an involuntary patient a full year after he first met me on that basis. Having lost the review board hearing, I was ordered to remain involuntary for an additional three months and given a new diagnosis: borderline personality disorder (BPD). An individual with BPD, I was told, typically exhibits five or more of the following symptoms: emotional instability, problems controlling anger, chaotic interpersonal relationships, fears of abandonment, identity disturbance, sense of emptiness, parasuicidal behavior or threats, impulsivity, dissociated responses, paranoid ideation, high sensitivity, and immediate and extreme reactions. I guess I qualify, with my violent anger spells, volatile relations with men, fears of rejection by family members, unstable sense of self, chronic feelings of emptiness, suicidal attempts, impulsive decision-making regarding sexual promiscuity, detached responses, mistrust of authority figures, extreme sensitivity, and mood instability.

Although some people newly diagnosed with BPD hate being squeezed into a diagnostic box, as do I, for me there is also great relief in learning that many of my adverse symptoms and behaviors can be subsumed under one disorder, that it affects other people as well, and that it is not a "life sentence." Indeed, I was told that with therapy and support, folks with BPD can learn to reshape negative modes of thinking and manage their impulses so they avoid saying and doing harmful things—information that assured me I can lead a happy and productive life as long as I work at it.

While on the one hand the light shed by this diagnosis brings some relief, on the other I am having trouble coping with Dr. Alexander's control over me. I am also racked with turbulence over the changes he has made, the extension of my involuntary status, and the extreme stress resulting from not being given the KOD, a solution I have come to rely on in times of unmanageable turmoil.

*August 29:* Since I was allowed to go for walks alone and longed to recreate the effects of the KOD drug, a few days ago I headed to the nearby drugstore and bought thirty-two sleeping pills. Then I wrote a letter explaining that I was not trying to commit suicide but if I died I was sorry for the pain it might cause my family. I called Lance to tell him I loved him, and being intuitive, Lance translated "I love you" into "I'm going to kill myself."

No sooner did I finish taking all the pills than an attendant came into my room saying, "Sara, your brother is concerned about you. So we are going to keep a close eye on you." As before, instead of sleeping I had hallucinations and couldn't walk or talk properly. While I hallucinated that my legs were turning black, the staff asked me what I had taken, but when I said, "Sleeping pills," Gary replied, "Sara, if you really took sleeping pills, then why are you awake?" I told them to retrieve the note I'd written, which stated exactly what I had taken, but they still would not believe me. Due to my behavior, I was again placed in CNC and, for the first time, given a bedpan to urinate in, as my door was to be locked at all times. Apparently the staff was unaware that my prolonged periods of confinement over the past year had given rise to an intense fear of seclusion.

It was the most frustrating night I ever experienced. Unable to cope with solitary confinement, I cried the entire time and banged on the door, pleading with the night attendant to let me out. Finally, in a desperate attempt to escape I asked if I could go to the bathroom instead of urinating in the pan, and once there I stalled, terrified that I might not be allowed out of my room again. When security came to force me back to my room, I huddled in a ball on the floor, rocking and crying. Although I told them I had an extreme phobia about men handling me, Gary began aggressively twisting my arm, and I retaliated instinctively by punching him in the nose. Within a heartbeat, six men had me in a cattle hold—face down, legs crossed, heels pressed against my butt. Enraged and helpless, I screamed, "I'll kill you!" Although I eventually calmed down and apologized for my behavior, I suspected this would not be the end of the incident.

When Dr. Alexander met with his team the next day, I was asked to attend. Immediately he pressured me into making a false confession: if I admitted to taking the thirty-two sleeping pills, I would be kept in CNC, but if I said I had taken fewer I would be released. Opting for liberation from solitary confinement, I invented a story about having taken just a few pills to get their attention. I felt ashamed to lie, yet learned firsthand how people can be pressured into making false confessions by folks who control them.

Two days later, I was charged with assault, and although the officer who served the papers told me I would probably not be sentenced to jail time if found guilty, I experienced great stress. My mother hired a criminal defense lawyer, who felt that I had been assaulted and had simply reacted to the use of force. The more I told him about how patients are humiliated, restrained, and confined within our region's mental health system, the more incredulous he became and agreed that it was as if I had been living in a world with its own laws. As we read the witness statements, I found them all to be accurate except two—one by a nurse who stated that I had attacked Gary without just cause (omitting the fact that he had previously twisted my arm) and the other by Dr. Alexander, who testified to my "sound state of mind" when the incident occurred.

The case ended up dividing the staff, some of whom believed I should be found guilty while others felt Gary should not have pressed charges. Further, the more my lawyer and I dug into Gary's past, the more we were convinced that he was anything but upstanding. A patient confided that Gary had had a sexual relationship with her years before, when she was a juvenile recently released from the psychiatric ward. In addition, an eighteen-year-old patient revealed that Gary had told her about a sexual dream he'd had about her. He had also made inappropriate comments to me after seeing pictures of me as a "bikini beer girl." Patients who knew Gary thought he was only pressing charges against me because I had hurt his ego by giving him a bloody nose.

Eventually the charges were dropped, but by then the stress had taken its toll on me. Not only was this a hollow victory, but from my vantage point it did little to change the treatment of hospitalized mental patients in the region. I was foolish to think it might.

*September 10:* My stress has increased exponentially, due to events that have exacerbated my increasingly fragile state. First, Julie was discharged, leaving me more isolated than ever. Next, Lance pulled away; I sensed he loved me less the healthier I became, a notion I found devastating. Then my period returned, making me feel like an eleven-year-old girl all over again, reexperiencing the emotional pain of this life transition. Not knowing what else to do, I burned myself with cigarettes, leaving ten ugly circular scars on my arm. It's strange to say, but a wave of relief washed over me as each burn bore into my skin, transferring my inner pain to the outside, where I could touch, hear, and see it. Externalizing my wretched pain gave me a little more control over my circumstances.

"Cutters," who practice a similar form of self-mutilation, say that when their blood flows it feels as if the "poison" or "bad" stuff inside them is being released and that the subsequent feeling of relief can become addictive. It's a sad commentary that good people have to hurt themselves to feel better. Hopefully, most of us have the strength and courage to confront our demons without misusing power against our bodies like others may have done to us.

*October 1:* Despite our forced separation, Julie and I developed a plan to see each other. Dr. Thirlwall, at last back from her vacation, had decided I could start receiving accompanied day passes out of the hospital, but my family lived hours away. So I asked her if I could have my Jeep brought down to give to Julie, necessitating a pass that would allow me to see her. And Lance, who had been using the Jeep, agreed to drive it down, assuring me that I would see him.

My first weekend with day passes went well. I had my left eyebrow pierced to celebrate the occasion and shopped with Lance, starting to feel a part of his life again. Later I realized that my conclusion about Lance's love diminishing as I became well did not reflect the truth. It had, in fact, been hard for Lance to watch someone he loved burn herself and be otherwise self-destructive, so out of self-preservation he had chosen to distance himself. Also, Lance had his own issues regarding our father's sexual abuse of me when we were children, perhaps feeling that he had failed to save his little sister. In addition, Lance realized that by supporting me he might be helping me maintain my illness, and it was indeed true that the more love and attention I received, the more I wanted to stay ill. I was caught in a vicious cycle.

Julie and I remained close, and I renewed my connection with a fellow patient named Marnie, whom I had met briefly during our prior treatment at the hospital. Since we had last seen each other, she had lost weight while I had gained 80 to 90 pounds, and had it not been for our similar sounding raspy voices, we might not have recognized each other. In any case, Marnie felt intuitively that Julie was using me and was a bad influence, whereas I myself was blind to Julie's effect on me. Whenever Julie and I went shopping, I would happily put her purchases on my credit card. And when Dr. Thirlwall allowed me to spend Saturday nights at Julie's home—our evenings turned to power drinking, pot smoking, and cocaine.

One particular night of partying changed our relationship in an unexpected way. Drinking led to drugs, dancing, kissing, then a three-some with Julie's husband Jack, although it seemed as if he was not present. After that, Julie and I started spending our Saturday nights at a hotel, at which point her dysfunctional marriage rapidly deteriorated. Although I am comfortable with the fact that I have had bisexual experiences, I look forward to living in the future as a straight woman, meeting a male soul mate, marrying, and having or adopting children.

*October 28:* Aware that my involuntary status is going to end November 12, Julie has decided to leave her husband, get a place with me on the beach, and bring her six-year-old son to live with us. In tandem with Dr. Thirlwall and my social worker, Nancy, I have been tackling my end of the arrangements. I plan to pay for this new beginning with money I received from my father last month as compensation for his earlier abuse.

This reparation came about because in May I finally asked Dr. Black for the mail my father had previously sent me. Within days, I received two letters that confirmed my memories. The following are excerpts from those letters:

> *I am writing you this note to apologize for what I did to you. For the last ten years or more, the memory of what happened has been blocked from my mind. I believe I experienced a major mental breakdown in the 1980s, and during this period I did things I don't understand. . . . I now believe that I did the thing you recall. I remember being on your mother's and my bed in "contact" with you, and looking at our wedding picture. . . . I recall waking up at*

*your Grammy's, feeling as though I had just had a sexual type*
*dream about you.* [This event, which happened the summer
before seventh grade, constitutes my last sexual abuse memory.] *I recall a dreamlike memory of being in the shower. . . . I*
*recall having inappropriate thoughts about you. . . . Please accept*
*my regrets for the sorrow I have caused you. And please, if you*
*can, forgive me.*

Upon reading my father's words of confession, I so admired his willingness to be honest and take responsibility for his actions that I allowed him
to visit. When he did, it became clear to me that he was unwell, but I was
angry and wanted him to pay—literally and figuratively! He agreed to
establish a trust fund for me. In August, I told him I didn't want a dime
from him, that no amount of guilt-infested money could ever make up for
the things he did to me, but come September he nevertheless gave my
mother a large sum of money for me. It wasn't a bribe to keep me from
pressing charges, he claimed, but rather a fund for my education and
future well-being. Of course, at that point no one really knew if I would
ever be competent enough to take care of myself.

Despite my ability to help pay for a new place to share with Julie, our
plans never materialized. I put money down on an apartment and was
ready for early discharge on November 1, but Julie disappeared and, upon
surfacing a week later, said her husband was threatening to take away her
son, and her family said they would disown her, if it was true that we were
lesbians. Venting her anger at me, she insinuated that I had made her gay
and convinced her to leave her husband. Regardless of the falsity of these
statements, it was over between us. I was so hurt that I started to run,
thinking that if I ran fast enough my pain would be left behind—but it
wasn't. Just as Julie had displaced her anger onto me, I started to do the
same with my father, angry because he was the reason I was such a
destroyed shell of a human being.

By now I was having suicidal thoughts again, but this time it seemed
only fair for him to die, too. As a child I had contemplated killing him, but
this was the first time I made a plan to do so. I signed out on a pass until
9:00 p.m., telling Marnie I was going to the mall. At the mall, I picked up

ephedrine, which accelerates the heart rate, and the only weapon I could legally purchase, a butcher's knife. Then I bought a six-pack of beer, and spent my last eight dollars on gas. On the road home, I sang, drank, and popped pills as I drove. When I approached a tollbooth penniless, the man said, "Early Merry Christmas," and let me through.

I quietly entered my father's house, and when he appeared in the kitchen I told him, "I am going to kill you and then myself." He just looked at me and said with a nervous laugh, "Sara, no you're not." Meanwhile the hospital had notified the police that I was missing. My mother and Lance phoned, and my father told them I was there but not to call the police; he just wanted time to talk with me. He couldn't stop saying, "I just want to spend the rest of my life making up for what I've done. Don't ruin your future by killing me." As he talked, I began to feel sorry for him. He lived in our family home alone, had no friends, and now my family had little to do with him. He had been forced, because of his breakdown, to retire from the job he loved and had decorated my room the same as when I was little—as if attempting to undo the harm he had caused.

My pain was so overwhelming that instead of killing him, I ran out of the house and started cutting myself with the knife. Finally, the police arrived, having been notified of my whereabouts by Lance and my mother. I dashed inside and told my father I wasn't going back to CNC. The police, including one woman officer, forced their way in and per-suaded me to drop the knife. I complied and urged, "I came here intending to kill my father, so charge me and take me to jail"—a place that seemed preferable to CNC. They replied, "You're not in trouble, but you need to go to the hospital emergency room for stitches." And so I said, maintaining an unusually calm demeanor, "Okay, but would it be all right if the woman officer handled me? I get scared and violent when men touch me." They agreed, and in fact the male officer called a second woman to help.

At the emergency room, I was stitched and placed on an electro-cardiograph because of the pills I had taken. The officers asked to search my purse and I consented, without thinking about a favor I had done for someone earlier that day: a patient with a drug addiction had bought weed and, after I talked him out of using, given it to me to pass on to Julie. The officer pulled out of my purse a big bud of marijuana, and the only thing I could think to say was, "Would you believe me if I told you it wasn't mine?" Whether they did or not, they flushed it, saying, "You have enough to deal with." They were right—I still had plenty of issues to confront before finding enough inner security to live in the outside world.

## CHAPTER FOURTEEN

# A New Beginning

$\mathcal{D}$*ay 75:* For the past fifty-seven days I have balanced my dietary intake with physical activity levels, an immense achievement that generates an unfamiliar sense of pride and confidence. In fact, as frightening as the prospect is, I am ready to leave my eating disorder persona behind—even if in the process I temporarily lose my sense of self or others no longer find me exceptional. My new identity will be an expression not of a disorder but of the obstacles I have surmounted. For example, it has become surprisingly easy to hold my own in difficult situations, thinking through possible responses rather than suddenly reacting in a destructive way. The more aware I am of having such internal controls, the more my decisions lead to wellness. Ironically, these months at my father's house are teaching me that lasting emotional and psychological changes come from within.

Physically, too, I am on the cusp of positive change. The shock to my system resulting from the extended periods of self-starvation followed by rapid weight gains through binge eating appears to have diminished, and my once-emaciated-then-engorged body seems receptive to finding a natural state of homeostasis. My muscle tone is gradually returning and the excessive stores of fat I accumulated are decreasing. I have also started physiotherapy for my back, because a bone density test showed I was at significant risk for osteoporosis, a deterioration of bone mass common among older women, female athletes, and young women with anorexia or bulimia nervosa. While these are only some of the impairments resulting from my illness, I am motivated to face whatever life throws my way, including lingering issues I need to address in order to have a healthier future.

As I sat in the emergency room cubicle awaiting my fate, with a police officer poised like a gargoyle at my bedside, I was alarmed to see that the person arriving to transport me back to the facility was the outrageous woman from the sheriff's department who four months before had treated me so horribly. I immediately confronted her regarding the callous insensitivity she had demonstrated during the previous crisis. The same cold eyes then connected with mine, and she replied, "I don't recall the situation you're talking about."

"Yeah, right," I thought. The long drive back was as silent as our original ordeal had been, only this time I knew that her atrocious opinions of me were fueled by ignorance rather than animosity.

Once back at the facility, I was turned over to the night attendants, who, since it was nearly midnight, placed me in CNC. This time I didn't say a word, but come morning, when Dr. Thirlwall made her rounds, I asked to speak with her. I explained to her that multiple opportunities to kill my father had produced some important insights—that I could never go through with it and that the anger I had toward *him* was killing *me*. Dr. Thirlwall nodded with apparent understanding then asked whether I would attempt to escape if she allowed me out of seclusion, to which I answered no. Aware of the pain and fear I associated with solitary confinement, she released me from CNC that morning. I cried tears of relief, feeling that we were on the same team, that she took my input seriously, and that saying no to impulsivity was a viable option for me.

On a more subliminal level, I was beginning to draw conclusions about isolation as a therapeutic measure. When seclusion, a brief measure, is used among patients who are at extreme risk to themselves or others, it may be beneficial, I decided; however, the prolonged isolation of human beings who are not overtly dangerous to themselves or others constitutes an insidious form of torture that kills the soul. It is better to place such individuals back into the mainstream with appropriate supervision and interventions.

I also deduced that just as isolation without proper treatment can ultimately intensify the behavior of a psychiatric patient prone to violence, putting a sex offender in jail without intensive efforts at rehabilitation may cause his illness to resurface with a vengeance upon his release back into society. For this reason I did not consider it advantageous to put my father in jail. Nor would I recommend leaving him alone with a child.

*November 4, 1999:* Due to the treatment I received in CNC under Dr. Black's care, I have developed a mild case of posttraumatic stress disorder (PTSD) complete with nightmares, flashbacks, and intense anxiety over being in proximity to environments resembling the cramped and confining quarters of that establishment. Consequently, revisiting the hospital proved to be exceptionally anxiety provoking, and adding to my distress was an acute fear of psychiatrists—coalescing in a constellation of symptoms reminiscent of those I experienced as a result of my childhood sexual abuse. My initial treatment has in essence retraumatized me, thus I must now heal not only from my eating disorders but from the treatment used to combat them.

Since my release from CNC, I have reached a turning point in my recovery. I now know that life will go on whether or not I'm here to enjoy it, so I might as well take part in it. After all, even my father has been able to move forward, starting a new job with a different company. In addition, Dr. Thirlwall has made it clear that I might require long-term care, in which case I'll be transferred to yet another psychiatric institution—a dreadful thought that compels me to get my act together. After this long, painful journey, it seems I am finally able to take responsibility for my recovery not because I am being forced to but because I want to.

*November 13:* Yesterday I was declared a voluntary patient under Dr. Thirlwall's care. The main catalyst for my enhanced functioning appears to be my deepening participation in psychotherapy with Dr. Kaye, the psychologist I have been working with over the past four months. She is exceedingly trustworthy and quite perceptive. One day, for example, she asked me to draw a picture of a person, then instantly observed, "Sara, I can see that you are strong willed, aggressive, and have poor self-esteem and a distorted body image." She had me dead-on. Dr. Kaye is also supportive and compassionate, laughing with me and calling me "Little One." In addition, she explains psychological dynamics and offers me self-help strategies, such as the following:

> Before making a decision, always ask yourself, "Is this going to help me or hurt me?"

> Remember the hot-air balloon theory: Express your anger in a healthy way or you'll keep blowing hot air till your balloon bursts.

> Bear in mind the ruts in a country road theory: As you drive along, your tires will keep getting stuck in the same ruts unless you deliberately steer your vehicle away from them.

The most profound support I have received from Dr. Kaye is intense dialectical behavior therapy (DBT), a self-management program developed by Marsha M. Linehan that helps individuals with borderline personality disorder (BPD) gain control over their self-destructive behaviors. According to Linehan's theory, people with BPD are born with an extremely high sensitivity and extreme reaction to emotional stimuli, have a slow recovery period, and grow up in invalidating and devaluing environments. As adults, they tend to be uncertain about their feelings and unable to mediate between various polarities. DBT teaches us to balance these polarities through a series of skills. As we gain proficiency in them, we progressively decrease our interpersonal chaos, our impulsiveness, confusion about the self, and emotional dysregulation.

A social worker and friend of the family gave me a somewhat different perspective on the success of DBT. She explained that it helps people with BPD reshape debilitating patterns of thought that originated in a childhood permeated by uncertainty, insecurity, and instability, which caused them to question their own feelings, beliefs, and social interactions. She also said that people diagnosed with BPD may have a genetic susceptibility to the disorder. In either case, to mitigate the unbearable stresses that come their way, people with BPD often seek relief, in part, by polarizing their experiences into categories of good and bad, such as the following:

I can trust her, but I can't trust him for a second.

This clinic is great; the last one was terrible.

This teacher is amazing; that one's awful.

I'm really awesome; (an hour later) I'm a hopeless mess.

Although polarizing our thoughts—"splitting" is the term some professionals use—removes uncertainty and temporarily reduces anxiety, the social worker added, it has a serious downside: it keeps us locked in an invented world of absolutes rather than adapting to a complex world in which people and situations are not black or white, but many shades of gray. (In fact, it was my penchant for splitting that destroyed many of my childhood relationships.) Over time, DBT helps us stop problematic splitting, enabling us to function immeasurably better and ultimately make a difference in life. It's also constructive, she said, to be around people who don't overreact when we do, but instead understand that we occasionally perceive reality as "all good or all bad."

*November 19:* In conjunction with individual therapy, I am participating in general group therapy and groups specializing in skills, self-esteem, and anger management. General group therapy provides an opportunity to learn about the diversity of people's problems, including alcoholism, drug addiction, and PTSD. In these sessions I have met men with PTSD resulting from either childhood molestation or war; businesspeople who have become workaholic; people struggling with their sexuality; parents with out-of-control children; teens and adults coping with the aftereffects of suicide attempts; individuals who lost fortunes to gambling addictions; people facing the loss of a loved one due to a tragic accident; individuals depressed because of incurable diseases; and men and women living in abusive relationships governed by everyday violence. Learning about the range of other people's problems helps me put my own in perspective.

In the skills group, we study distress tolerance—through self-soothing techniques—and mindfulness. Three methods have been introduced to assist us: (1) choosing wisely by listing pros and cons before making important decisions; (2) developing a "Teflon mind" that permits feelings,

thoughts, and experiences to flow in and out without causing a disturbance, something I'm practicing with regard to my sexual abuse memories; and (3) allowing for life in the moment, paying attention to the here
and now, and not worrying about the past or future, a method I use to
quiet my racing thoughts.

In the self-esteem group, we are exploring the familiar question "Do
you see the glass as half full or half empty?" As a result of these new
perspectives, I try looking for the positive in situations and in myself,
realizing that self-esteem is based not only on how I view myself physically
but on how I regard myself as a person. In the past, I was so used to being
seen, by myself and others, as manipulative, dishonest, abusive, violent,
and anorexic that I forgot how creative I could be, and how funny, generous, empathetic, and loyal, as well. One of the self-esteem facilitators took
this idea further, telling us: "Life really isn't what you see, it's what you
perceive. For example, if you perceive yourself as a manipulator it will
bring you down, but if you perceive yourself as a courageous person who
has cultivated an impressive array of skills to stay safe and get your needs
met, you will walk proud. Perceiving moves us from observation to understanding, so that suddenly the glass is neither half full nor half empty, but
overflowing."

In the anger management group, I am learning to distinguish between
fight and flight and to identify different expressions of anger, such as
masking or stuffing, exploding, or chronic upset. A person experiencing
anger can either let it out constructively to work through it or hold on
to it, which results too often in abusive behaviors and lost relationships.
For me, the most important anger management technique we practice
is ways of altering our communication; rather than verbally attacking
someone, I am learning to communicate in a nonthreatening manner.
All these groups give me resources that will help me finally take owner-
ship of my future.

*December 2:* After becoming a voluntary patient, I decided to get back in
shape. So over the past two weeks, in addition to all the therapy, I started
doing yoga and toning in the morning, taking three thirty-minute walks a
day, riding a stationary bike when possible, and doing gymnastics and

dance on weekends. Dr. Thirlwall, aware that I am again becoming obsessive about exercise, has refused to limit my activities, believing things will normalize on their own now that I seem more accountable for my decisions. I credit the faith she has placed in my self-contained ability to heal—as opposed to Dr. Black's ongoing directives—for inspiring my newly found motivation to recover. As predicted, balance eventually did materialize within my routine.

I also have been working with a dietitian, Lisa, to eat three balanced meals a day and one small nighttime snack, all of which I ensure are low in calories and fat-free. The most difficult treat to pass up is chocolate, which, when consumed, does wonders for depression. A popular joke around here is "Who's up for having sex?"—a euphemism for eating chocolate.

One big temptation in this regard is the high-fat foods available at our D-Day (Discharge Day) parties. Marnie, a patient named Tanya, and I throw these parties for recovered patients on the night before they are to be discharged. We decorate a common area with balloons and streamers; set out platters of pizza, bowls of chips, and a frosted cake; then gather in the room and surprise the patient. After eating, we watch a movie, our two favorites of which are *What About Bob,* a hilarious film in which a patient drives his psychiatrist crazy, and *Patch Adams,* about a doctor who uses humor to heal his patients. Although we gather to say good-bye and boost morale, we attempt to meet these objectives by devouring comforting foods—a dynamic that has unfortunately gotten the best of me, triggering a return to bingeing. Now, even when we're not partying, Tanya orders a pizza for us to binge on, after which she purges and I, envying her, try vomiting. One night last week I purged in the shower and, having clogged the drain, had to confess to my nurse. A binge tonight brought on food poisoning, which I interpret as a warning against this destructive behavior.

*December 8:* I have taken a turn for the worse, slipping into a depression. Things started to tailspin a few nights ago while a group of us were waiting for the television to be freed up so we could watch a movie. According to the rules, if a movie is not started by 10:00 p.m., we are not allowed to see it. So around 9:00 p.m., after a few hours of waiting, the others persuaded me to approach the elderly woman who had been monopolizing the screen. I did, whereupon she yelled, "Just because you practically live here doesn't mean you own the place." This cruel reference to my prolonged treatment felt like a knife slashing my heart, and I screamed, "Take it back; I don't live here. Take it back; this isn't my home." She was right, however: I did live in a psychiatric unit and had to face the implications.

*December 19:* Last Monday over breakfast, Tanya and I asked each other if we were sick of life and wished we didn't have to live anymore. We both answered yes and made a plan to take our lives. Having attempted to commit suicide numerous times before, we were experts in what didn't work, so this time we opted for what would work. We took turns going to nearby drugstores to accumulate a massive supply of sleeping pills. Tanya located a hotel where we could go that didn't demand an ID or credit card. We then decided to each write a suicide letter to take with us. We agreed that it seemed comforting to not be alone during our final moments on earth.

This morning, while preparing to embark on our adventure, I sat down to write my letter but suddenly realized that my words portrayed a will to live, and that if I refrained from acting impulsively, in a few days my life would seem different. An hour later, when I got together with Tanya as planned, I told her that instead of taking our lives we could help each other fight our illnesses, and she agreed. Having chosen life, I gave the pills to Dr. Thirlwall and vowed to never again make important decisions impulsively.

*December 27:* As Christmas approached, I decided to celebrate with a three-day visit to Jackie rather than staying at my mother's house, the site of an earlier suicide attempt. The night before leaving for Jackie's house, I received an unexpected gift from a former patient named Lana, a nineteen-year-old now enrolled as a photography student at Mount Allison University. It was a tape entitled "Sara's Song," which she had written then recorded in a studio—a present I found touching and inspirational.

Elated by Lana's thoughtfulness, I took full advantage of Christmas as a chance to bond with Jackie and her husband Devan, as well as get to know my nephew Tanner. Then during our gift exchange, I gave my entire family a candle with money hidden inside and a note on angel paper that read:

*To my angels on earth~*

*I often thought about becoming an angel to all of you. I thought that comfort was in heaven, but 'tis the season to find true peace on earth, and that lies in being around my family. I often thought that if I were in heaven I could offer you the gift of my eternal spirit to protect and guide you through this journey called life. But as appealing as heaven may seem, it lacks one necessity for survival and happiness—my family. You have been my backbone, my number-one fans and cheerleaders. I love and appreciate everything you have done for me:*

*Janice, who gave me the Serenity Prayer, to help me have the courage to change the things I can and to accept the things I cannot.*

*Jackie and Devan, who on their honeymoon to Disneyland bought me a giant Tigger to remind me that "Tiggers always bounce back."*

*Lance, who when I wanted to be a sunflower but felt like a dandelion reminded me that dandelions always open up and let go of their baggage.*

*Mom, who has been more loyal than the mail carrier, always there regardless of my "weather."*

*And my nephew Tanner, my spiritual guide and voice of reason, with his advice, "Sara, come in car to my house and bring presents."*

*For Christmas this year, your gift is myself, alive and with you for the holidays. Remember that I am always with you. When you need or miss me, light the candle, see the glow and the shadows all around the room, and watch the flame dance . . . that's me. The money in the candle represents partial repayment to you for the investment of love and kindness you have given me. But my real repayment will be by becoming the best friend, sister, sister-in-law, mother, and aunt I*

*can be. Please leave a candle lit so I can see my way, because one day*
*I am coming home!*

Everyone was moved except Lance, who assumed the letter meant I was going to kill myself in the future. But that was not my intention.

Although I had no difficulty eating Christmas dinner, I did have a problem on the drive back to the hospital with Mom the next day. We stopped at a trucker's restaurant for lunch, and when I saw how large the portions were, I started to cry. My mother brought me back to reality, saying, "Just eat what you want and leave the rest." Instantly I realized that I still had Dr. Black's program etched into my subconscious, especially the rule to eat what was served to me.

*December 30:* No sooner did I start making plans for New Year's Eve 2000 than Dr. Thirlwall offered me a night pass out with Tanya. And so I was eagerly looking forward to bringing in the new year—until this afternoon, when I went clothes shopping and couldn't find a cute dress in a size 12 suitable for a person my age. Apparently women in this society are prisoners of the media, which constantly equate being beautiful with being thin. Captivated by models who reinforce the notion that thin is beautiful, we nearly die attempting to achieve such a goal ourselves. How much saner it would be to present women with diverse fashions and models of different sizes and shapes.

*January 14, 2000:* When people comment on my weight gain, telling me I look healthy, I respond, "I *feel* healthy, too." In my mind, weight is currently connected to nothing other than health and well-being. In fact, now that I've stopped associating food with body image, I've been eating three healthy meals a day and losing weight without making an effort.

*January 26:* This entire month I have been focusing on my mental health, taking full advantage of the system, since I am to be discharged at the end of the month. During this time I met a young man named Seth, but we decided it was too soon to be dating each other. When Seth eventually began dating another patient, I was hurt but knew if we were meant to be together we would find our way back into each other's lives.

I've recently gained a new perspective on death, too, viewing it as a natural occurrence in life and something never to be tampered with, as our time
on earth is precious. Further, I've seen how tragic the death of a loved one
can be for the living. The realization came sharply into focus this morning,
when I received a call from Tanya's mother saying Tanya had attempted to
take her life and was in critical care. She had told her mother that she was
going to see a movie with me yesterday and then never returned home last
night. Because she was found at the hotel where we had planned to die
together, I feel partly responsible, having initially agreed to our plan. Following my change of heart, I had sent her sunflowers and said a few prayers,
but we never did speak again, for I felt I had to focus on self-preservation.

On a brighter note, my mother and Janice have been making weekend
trips to help me find an apartment to rent in the city, where assistance will
be close by if I need it. Together we settled on a two-bedroom unit on the
top floor of a large brick building with a pool, sauna, and friendly land-
lord. The apartment has a patio and picture window facing the sunrise,
which curiously feels like home. But as excited as I am to embark on my
new life of freedom, I also have many fears—of living in an unstructured
environment, failure, loneliness, lack of safety and support, managing
everyday stress, living in a strange city alone, responsibility, working,
facing the world as an overweight woman, making friends and dating,
and resuming the role of an adult.

*January 30:* Today, two years after entering the hospital, I am free at last.
This morning I presented the staff with a thank-you poem composed for
the occasion by Janice. Then Dr. Kaye and I discussed her plan to transfer
me to day therapy with psychologist Tracey Mathers, as well as to day
therapy groups. I felt pride in how far I'd come and was more certain than
ever that I could put the past to rest and live a more fulfilling life in the
future. As I left Dr. Kaye's office, she presented me with a card she had
made that read, "Remember the message of the sunflower: 'Face the sunshine and the shadows will fall behind.'"

On my way out of the hospital, I was told to pick up a surprise at the
gift shop. There I found sunflowers, and a card bearing the words "I knew
you could do it. Love, Mom."

## CHAPTER FIFTEEN

# Redefined Relationships

*Day 82:* The meager connection I have forged with my father is surely as good as it's going to get. Like wounded soldiers in the aftermath of battle, we are dazed and depleted, seemingly incapable of mustering up energy to discuss the past and move on to a better future. We do little to inspire each other's trust, and our communication is sparse, composed almost exclusively of my father's expressions of regret and my assurances of forgiveness, which I somehow correlate with gaining momentum to move forward. But despite the superficiality of our discussions, they have exceeded my expectations. The honesty and vulnerability we both display make it clear we are real people to each other and that our feelings matter. As much as I hate what he did to me, I would rather have him in my world, anchoring our reconfigured relationship, than absent from it.

I have also begun reexamining relationships with my care team under the directorship of Dr. Black. Just today I visited the hospital in my hometown and felt old pangs of abandonment and betrayal; I emerged joyous, however, having accessed a new insight and witnessed the birth of my sister's baby girl. Upon first stepping through the entryway of the hospital, I headed for the cafeteria, where I spotted Tina and Eve—my former nurse and dietitian, respectively—on their lunch break. They greeted me with a warm embrace, and I exuberantly proclaimed, "I am well. Anorexia nervosa is curable."

They appeared pleased about my recovery, but refrained from taking credit for it. I suspected that neither staff member felt good about the treatment I received under their care, a hunch that was confirmed when Tina whispered in my ear, "It was the *other* place that helped you, wasn't it?"

As tempted as I was to agree with her, I flashed on the idea that without the support of Dr. Black's patient care team I would never have survived anorexia well enough to have eventually recovered from it. "Actually, you saved my life," I told her.

Looking in the windows of the psychiatric ward stirred up more unforeseen emotions. Like an older teen leaving the nest for the first time, when I was newly discharged I had vacillated between enthusiasm and apprehension, all the while struggling with an acute sense of abandonment and betrayal. Today, peeking into this cocoon of nurturance and safety made me yearn for it once again, especially when I saw staff members who had cared for me now taking care of others. "Don't you still love me?" I cried inside. "Why did you let me go?" The feeling that I was no longer an important part of their lives triggered painful memories of worrying about my mother's love for me as my days of being institutionalized dragged on. "Now that I am out of her sight," I would ask myself, "am I also out of her mind?"

I hurried along to labor and delivery, where the birth of my beautiful niece transformed my understanding of the effects of trauma on the young and, by extrapolation, the impact of my own past on my future. While gazing at this precious newborn, I reflected on the fact that children are never born bad though they can, if influenced by a negative environment, develop unwanted behavior. Then I called to mind men and women raised in abusive households who chose never to be abusive themselves. In effect, witnessing the miracle of new life removed the indelible blot I had affixed to the future of anyone raised in a violent setting. Victims of abuse can actually make excellent choices in life, I concluded. In seeing beyond my father's badness to the good inherent in everyone makes me aware *in my bones* that a bad history can become a good incentive for change.

Sadly, before the end of my first week in the new apartment, old patterns resurfaced. I began obsessively dieting, cleaning, and exercising, all the while feeling euphoric, as if on an independence high. I also started dating Seth, but our relationship quickly fizzled, primarily because, due to a previous involvement with drugs, dealers were following him around the city, threatening him and people associated with him. Eventually, after holding his sister and mother hostage at gunpoint, the men were sentenced to prison. Another reason Seth and I broke up was because we held opposing views on life and thus approached it very differently. He preferred to sit on the sidelines, while I liked to play in the game. I resolved to wait for Mr. Right, even if it meant years of solitude.

At about this time I purchased my first computer, hoping to find a link to companionship. Although I had reservations about meeting people over the Internet, I hungered for conversations with people who weren't patients; yet making friends in the outside world had proved to be difficult, due partly to the stigma associated with my illness and also to my sense that the world didn't understand me. Marnie, who lived two hours away and stayed with me three days a week to attend day therapy, and John, a nineteen-year-old patient, were the only true friends I had.

*February 16, 2000:* Today I quit day therapy after attending a journal group session where we were given a list of twenty-eight topics and asked to write about one for fifteen minutes. The list included three tragic-sounding topics, one or another of which everyone but me chose to write about. I selected a positive topic: "I am proud of myself because . . ." After I read my essay, the group leered at me as if I had no idea what it was like to be depressed and ill. Even though I am again dieting and exercising in obsessive ways, I have been feeling a healthier attitude emerging from somewhere deep inside me, so I wrote these words:

> *I am proud of myself because . . . I kept on fighting the biggest battle I may ever have to face. After being hospitalized for two long years, I was finally released on January 30, 2000. So many times I wanted to give up along the way but somehow prevailed. Initially, I thought it was up to the professionals to cure me, but then I realized I was part of the team and had to do the work. I was able to finally surrender to therapy and start loving myself, believing that I deserved to get better now and have respect for myself and a new perspective on life. I have vowed never to regard suicide as an option or solution. I plan to live life to my fullest potential. I hope my strug-*

*gles can be an inspiration to others who have felt as hopeless and lost*
*as I have. I promise you, where there is a will there is a way.*

My decision to leave day therapy was prompted by a desire to acceler-
ate my recovery. Although psychotherapy groups and skill-building classes have kept me alive, especially in times of being clinically depressed or
suicidal, they also keep me occupied with personal problem solving—
which translates into spending hours a day dwelling on my flaws and
defects. A group leader once told me that focusing on "doing" as opposed
to simply "understanding" can help me build confidence by directing my
attention to things I'm doing *right* rather than all that's gone wrong. My
intention now is not to turn my back on those who mirror my weaknesses, but to increase my exposure to people and situations that exercise my
strengths.

*March 11:* I have been biking daily for at least eight hours. Also, I have
been starving myself all day and eating all night. Although this time my
binge eating has more to do with physical as opposed to emotional
hunger, the obsession must be overcome if I am to attain balance and
health. With this in mind, today I joined a local gym and started working out under the supervision of a personal trainer. I plan to adhere to
her program: following rules about what to eat, recording the foods I
consume each day, counting calories, logging output for the day, and
having weekly weigh-ins.

As time passed, it became evident that the program was instigating
behavior very similar to my former anorexic routines. I was in the gym
every day, restricting my food intake, feeling guilty about eating, and
unable to so much as stroll in the park without calculating the number of
calories I was burning. One day after stepping on the scale and crying
because I had not lost enough pounds that week, I knew I had to quit. It
was a landmark decision I had felt inspired to make because although I
was hurting I had a new companion: self-awareness.

*April 23:* A few hours ago I declared myself "recovered" and no longer in
need of medication. Feeling stabilized for over a month now, I have come

to the conclusion that the antidepressant, antianxiety, and sleep medications I have been taking preserve the "mentally ill" label I am trying to shed. Secretly, I am hoping that without the meds my illness will go away entirely.

It didn't take long for me to learn the dangers of stopping medication prematurely. At first, unlike most people who slip into a low mood when they go off antidepressants, I felt euphoric. I began spending beyond my means, became promiscuous, got up at 4:00 a.m. every morning to cycle and lift weights while enjoying the sunrise, and danced the night away, either at home alone or out at a club. My self-esteem was so enhanced that I wore tight leather pants and tops that barely covered my once A-cup, now D-cup breasts. Having lost my sense of appropriate behavior, I had no idea that my actions were extreme and inviting ridicule. Out of touch with appropriate protocols, I made some terrible decisions, such as going to the home of a strange man and having unprotected sex.

Eventually, Dr. Thirlwall suggested that the cause for my irrational behavior may not have been the abrupt cessation of medications but rather a new, underlying illness: bipolar disorder. One day when my mother had accompanied me to an appointment, Dr. Thirlwall recommended that we read the book *An Unquiet Mind* by Kay Redfield Jamison, who suffered from manic depression, commonly known as bipolar disorder. Much to my dismay, I recognized many parallels between her erratic lifestyle and my own. Dr. Thirlwall determined that I indeed demonstrated bipolar traits, and she placed it on my psychiatric "radar screen" as something to be watched closely.

Learning that I might be grappling with bipolar disorder did little to curb my rash behavior. On the contrary, I began engaging in risky sexual activities with a handsome man from my apartment building, then woke up one morning fully cognizant of the fact that I detested casual sex. When I approached him to put an end to our escapades, I discovered that all along he had wanted a relationship with me. So we dated for a week, at which point I saw that although he was good-looking from the outside, he was ignorant, narrow-minded, and racist on the inside. I questioned my criteria for choosing a partner, reevaluated my relationship priorities, and determined never again to forsake my personal values in exchange for having a man in my life.

*May 31:* A few weeks ago I started to spiral downhill again. Desperate to hold on, I sought help from alternative methods such as palm and tarot card readings, color therapy, chakra balancing, as well as gemstones and essential oils with healing properties. Although some of these sessions were momentarily soothing, I continued to suffer both physically and spiritually.

In my quest for self-esteem, energy, and peace, I finally went to a hypnotist. He told me to confess my fears, desires, and needs to the many spirits he claimed surrounded me, including one named Safari, who specialized in journeys. In response, I divulged the following:

*Fears:* Never loving myself, losing hope, being controlled, not losing weight, being alone forever, never letting go of the past, never succeeding in life, never finding my purpose, being rejected, dying before having had a chance to make a difference in the world.

*Desires:* Companionship, friendship, weight loss, understanding of my purpose in life, self-love, a soul mate, travel, giving back by helping others.

*Needs:* Courage, strength, self-control, acceptance, confidence, inner peace.

After five hypnotherapy sessions in his home, I began suffering from anxiety and depression. The hypnotist told me I had emotional blockage in my root chakra (pubic area) and that to heal me he wanted to pass cleansing energy through that area, a procedure that translated into a man touching my pubic area while I was in a vulnerable state. Aspects of the "cleansing"—his touch, the home setting, his statements that love is unconditional, and his insistence that I am special and loved—instantly triggered old memories of sexual abuse. Horrified that I had not checked his credentials in advance and that I had submitted to such a procedure outside of an office setting, where an attendant would have been present, I vowed never to return.

This morning I spent hours skipping stones across a placid pond, imagining the outcome of each one as an effect of the sexual abuse I endured as a child. The ripples they produced in the water represented the bad moves I had made in my life; their crash landings at rock bottom reminded me of the results of my bad decisions. Suddenly I wondered what it might be like to throw a stone and hope for a *positive* ripple. Closing my eyes, I tried to picture a *series* of positive ripples, and soon I could see small life changes rippling into magnificent solutions.

Returning home with a promise to bring order and balance to my life, I composed the following list of small changes to make each day.

### Reclaiming My Health—Body, Mind, and Soul

(1) Write down one positive aspect about yourself, and one person, place, and thing to be grateful for.

(2) Eat wholesome foods, because it makes your body feel good. Strive for normal eating patterns, and listen to what your body is telling you.

(3) Go step by step, without obsessing. For instance, feel good about cleaning just one room rather than the entire apartment.

(4) Find your purpose through studying or doing volunteer work.

(5) Jot down affirmations and recite them aloud.

(6) Meditate and pray at night.

(7) Practice abstinence.

(8) Dress in clothes that make you feel comfortable.

(9) Be kind to someone you don't know. Give money to charity, circulate positive energy to a stranger, or donate clothes you no longer wear.

(10) Plan an adventure for the near future, such as hiking, canoeing, or rappelling.

My life did improve, but the catalyst for this change was an unexpected event: my friend Anna, unaware that I was living in Moncton, moved to town to be near her sister. Our out-of-the-blue reunion, commemorating our shared love for adventure and nature, awakened great happiness within me.

*June 27:* Last week I took Anna back home to visit my family, despite an overwhelming feeling that I was not yet stable enough to sleep in my mother's house or withstand the community's comments about me. I went because I had promised Anna we would go and because my mother had been expecting us. Right away the trip evolved into a disaster. Upon arriving at my mother's house, I displaced a boatload of pent-up anger onto an undeserving Anna, crying, slamming doors, refusing to leave the house, and generally making our time together very unpleasant. I apologized, but she decided to cut the visit short. As she boarded the bus to visit her parents, Anna looked wistfully in my direction and, with genuine sympathy, said I had done well considering the circumstances. Profoundly moved by her message of forgiveness, my whole being resonated with the understanding that I have no right to inflict my grief on others.

Of all my relationships undergoing redefinition, this one sparked the most dramatic effects. Anna ultimately decided to live with her parents, and again I was alone, but this time I began looking for the strength to feel good about myself from the inside out. I had witnessed firsthand the terrible consequences of pleasing others—being a "good friend" and a "good daughter"—so I could feel good inside. This pattern, however, not only caused me to resent the people I was trying to please but left me struggling futilely to absorb happiness from the outside in, an impossible feat. My reunion with Anna taught me that by allowing positive emotions to take the place of the abuse inside me, I could learn to love myself and fully embrace my life.

## CHAPTER SIXTEEN

# LOST TO INSANITY

*D*ay 89: I have come to accept that life is forever changing and that we are free to either embrace or flee from our potential for growth. I am also aware that I could not move forward to even glimpse my potential for growth without directly confronting my past. *I had to return to my father's house.* For years I'd been down on myself for squandering people's efforts to make me well, and living with my father has given me a perfect chance to use the wisdom and skills they imparted. Their efforts, combined with the clarity I have achieved while living with my father, have produced within me a seed of hope: a vision of my future self as a courageous, confident, evolving woman who will draw strength from having overcome her anorexic identity.

Emerging slowly from the grip of insanity, I can see that just as I have changed, so too has my father. Lately he has stopped regurgitating past regressions during our time together; instead, he now focuses on the present and occasionally dares to peek into the future. Perhaps now that I have fully accepted the role of survivor, he no longer feels compelled to treat me as a victim. And by mutually allowing our hold on the past to diminish, we have begun functioning together in the here and now. Although we often disagree, we don't let any resulting tension disrupt our mending relationship. Still, we appreciate that our living arrangement, like all else, will not last forever. When the time is right, I feel confident that I will leave behind the security of my father's house and start a life of my own.

As if to reiterate the importance of change for continued growth, earlier today I received a small package from a friend's mother. Inside was a sunflower key chain and a letter that read: "Life is a series of changes. . . . Many times we must be willing to close the door on things familiar and let them go in order to fully embrace something new and strange. In new surroundings and circumstances, we discover previously unknown things about ourselves that lead to a richer and fuller life. Let peace be your companion as you explore this 'new' world."

After my disastrous trip home with Anna, I returned to what I considered my real home, my apartment in Moncton, certain that I could handle the change. I was glad to be back at my place, where I could find comfort, happiness, bliss, and inner peace. The town I grew up in, by contrast, brought out a side of me still rife with anger, frustration, low self-esteem, self-hate, and insecurity—all feelings that led to my eating disturbances and attempts to end my life. I was saddened to discover that not even the happiness I felt in Anna's presence could subdue the lifelike demons that still dwelled in my hometown. After she relocated, however, I was to discover that no one can give you inner peace and happiness; you must find them within yourself and then share them with others.

*July 2, 2000:* I am feeling pressured to discover my purpose in life. For years I have dreamed about somehow helping others, about giving back after all this receiving. To see if I was strong enough to cast myself in a sustained helping role, I recently decided to apply for work as an EMT (emergency medical technician). So after breakfast this morning, I went to register for a course on becoming a paramedic, an occupation that saves lives and helps others in a meaningful way. On my application form, I wrote:

> *It seems that everything we experience in life leads us in the direction we were meant to go. For me to feel successful and happy in a career, I therefore need to be in a profession that awakens within me this sense of a higher purpose, preferably through contributing to the*

*community and feeling connected to it. I could never work for finan-*
*cial gain alone, because I base success on how many people I have*
*been able to help. I enjoy being challenged on all levels: physically,*
*intellectually, emotionally, and spiritually. I have a quick and sharp*
*mind, and I like the stimulation of change. I'm intelligent and a fast*
*learner with a thirst for knowledge acquired through both theory*
*and hands-on experience. Perhaps one characteristic others agree on*
*is my stubbornness, but because of this quality I work hard and*
*never give up . . .*

Suddenly I had to set down my pen. Next thing I knew, I was in the
throes of a debilitating anxiety attack and had to be rushed to the emergency center. The anxiety, I later determined, had stemmed from learning
from an inside source that my chances of being accepted into the course
were slim because the required medical exam included a mental health
history. I was devastated to learn that the stigma attached to being an
ex–mental patient would prevent me from getting the position and testing
my strength to pursue my dreams. Seeing myself as an incompetent failure with no future, I started spiraling into a depression—my worst and
final bout.

*August 7:* I am knee-deep in a negative cycle of feelings and eating behaviors (see figure 6) stemming from contemptible thoughts about my body.
I think I am fat, ugly, and unworthy of love. I also think I can find love and
acceptance through weight loss, as I did when I was acutely anorexic and
starving for love. But no amount of caloric restriction seems to be enough,
so I turn to food, believing it will comfort me. Unable to control this gluttonous behavior, I think I am bad and punish myself by hiding away in my
apartment and exercising for hours on end.

To avoid the perils of prolonged isolation, I have been spending
weekends with my mother and Janice at their summer trailers in a beautiful park near the beach. There I have access to a pool, a playground, a
country-style diner, and facilities for barbecues and campfires. But even in
this vacation atmosphere I feel like I'm just existing rather than living. At
night I listen to the sounds of laughter coming from around the campfires

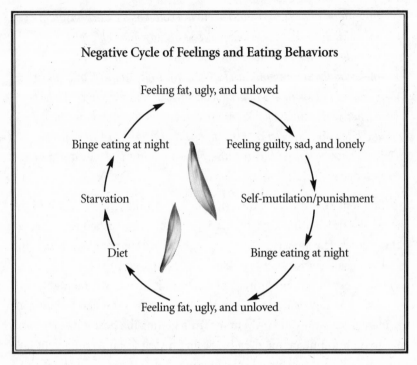

*Figure 6*

and wonder if I will ever be surrounded by friends drinking cold beer on a hot summer's night, roasting marshmallows, and laughing at stories about the "good old days."

*August 23:* While I was at my mother's and Janice's trailers last weekend, Jackie and three-year-old Tanner came to visit. On Saturday afternoon we went to the park, where the neighborhood children affixed themselves to me like glue, having me push them on the swings and play with them on the monkey bars. As delighted as I was, a wave of grief washed over me at the thought that I was so overweight, unattractive, and mentally deranged that I might never have children of my own. Turning to watch Jackie and Tanner, I began to envy her for having a family she loved and who loved her back. When she tried to console me by saying, "You're just at a different point in your life," all I heard was "different," which I took to mean I wasn't normal and would never have a sane, balanced life.

That weekend I also had to face my past in another way. I had nightmares and kept waking Jackie up as I screamed and talked in my sleep. The nightmares were related to my childhood sexual abuse, and I despaired about whether I could ever rid myself of those memories. As a result, it became increasingly clear that to have a future free of night terrors and daytime anxiety, I must actively make peace with my father and then let the past go.

*August 30:* For nearly two months, I have suffered from daily panic attacks. Most last only a few minutes, although some go on much longer. Typically, panic attacks, which sufferers occasionally mistake for heart attacks, can be triggered by social situations, phobias, mental illnesses, caffeine, illegal drugs, or alcohol. Symptoms include heart palpitations, breathing difficulties, out-of-body experiences, hot and cold flashes, sweating, difficulty swallowing, chest pain and pressure, and feelings of disorientation. Although panic attacks can usually be controlled with self-talk and medication, I had been too far out of touch with reality to help myself.

Compounding the difficulty, I have also been besieged by other problems. My OCD has been acting up, causing me to shave off every hair on my body, including my eyebrows, though not the hair on my head, and to scrub my body with SOS Soap Pads, frequently drawing blood. I have developed extremely surreal delusions: my legs appear to be black, my face swollen, the trees out my window made of gray paper. I am suffering from paranoia, which is provoking irrational beliefs that I am allergic to medications, nuts, oils, seeds, and food coloring. In short, I am living in fear. And being suspicious of pills, I am unable to quell this litany of severe symptoms with antianxiety and antipsychotic medications.

Worse, my visits to the emergency center are aggravating and counterproductive. On my first visit, I was given a blood test and a chest X-ray, but once the doctor discovered my mental history he dismissed my problems as being psychosomatic. Subsequently, every time I returned I was diagnosed as having had a panic attack and sent home without treatment, although my symptoms were worsening to the point where I had difficulty swallowing, keeping my balance, and hearing. Finally, I went to a medical center and did not reveal my mental history, whereupon the doctor, immediately after examining my throat and ears, diagnosed a bad virus and asked why I had let it get so out of hand.

During these months of anxiety, food has been a source of comfort and distraction, turning me, much to my disgust, into a 185-pound compulsive eater. This development rounded out my medical profile, depicting a person who suffered from every major eating disorder: anorexia nervosa, bulimia nervosa, binge eating, and now compulsive eating. While binge eating involves consuming a large amount of food within a short time—generally followed by purging or using laxatives, or excessive exercising—compulsive eating entails eating continuously, whether hungry or not, without attempting to undo the "damage." I find compulsive eating more disturbing than anorexia because of the intense feelings it evokes of being unable to gain control, a sensation similar to being sexually abused.

I feel hopeless, thinking that I will always have one eating disorder or another, and also frustrated at how differently compulsive eating and anorexia are treated. When I was anorexic, mental health workers hastened to control my illness; compulsive eating, on the other hand, is dismissed as my problem. Actually, both losing and gaining weight at a rapid pace are dangerous to health, and all eating disorders are psychological illnesses that should be treated with equal importance.

*September 7:* As if my life were not challenging enough, I have developed yet another disorder: a combination of social phobia and agoraphobia. A person suffering from a social phobia is usually aware that her fears are irrational and yet is unable to face the situations causing extreme distress, such as crowds, strangers, or unfamiliar environments. Agoraphobia is an abnormal fear of being helpless in embarrassing or unacceptable situations and thus involves avoiding public places. In grappling with both these phobias, I avoid all situations that cause me distress.

Unable to leave my apartment, I call my mother as often as twenty times a day, telling her I am dying. This afternoon she said, "Sara, I can't help you from this far away. You are not competent to live alone. Maybe it's time to come home." I was devastated by the possibility of having to spend the rest of my life being cared for.

To gain more clarity about my circumstances, I am using techniques I learned in therapy. For example, I just completed a Death vs. Life list to come to an informed decision about my future (see figure 7).

---

### Death vs. Life

| Death | Life |
|---|---|
| 1. I will never love myself or feel secure, so I will forever lack a sense of acceptance, esteem, and confidence. | 1. I have a family. |
| 2. I will never have a career, due to "psychiatric stigma." | 2. I want to write a book. |
| 3. I will never have friends, because I am too inadequate. | 3. I want to help others and know I can do so by first helping myself. |
| 4. I will never have a partner, because I feel unworthy of love. | |
| 5. My body is damaged beyond repair, sexually and physically (metabolism, back, scars). | |
| 6. I will always have an eating disorder, OCD, and BPD. | |
| 7. I am physically, mentally, emotionally, and spiritually depleted. | |

---

*Figure 7*

**September 11:** It remains difficult for me to let go of the past and allow myself to heal. My heart throbs with pain and anger, showing no hint of acceptance or forgiveness. I am in such despair that I can't imagine waking up one day without an eating disorder. Nor can I create balance or find peace in my life. I will never be able to love and give to others; after all, I do not love myself and I have nothing left to offer society. I can find no purpose in life, having lost my faith in a higher being. In addition, I am blind to the abundance in the world and no longer grateful for blessings in my life.

My only path to salvation is to confront my past directly. I will return home to live with the man and in the house where my problems all began, viewing this move as a symbolic suicide.

## CHAPTER SEVENTEEN

# Found at Last

*Day 100:* Being back home confronting my past in order to free myself for a better future has led not only to a new relationship with my father but to a kind of spiritual rebirth. I used to regard myself as a person lost in a war zone of sexual abuse and eating disorders, with always the same commands, to shoot or to surrender; now I see how illusory and self-generated that world really was. Having stepped outside it, I know in my bones that my true identity has meaning and purpose, and that boundless options lie before me.

For instance, I am now able to experience acceptance, which is nothing like craving approval, and to distinguish disagreement from rejection. I can release anger and feel joy. I recognize that mental illness is as real and serious as physical illness, and that no brain is immune to disease. Best of all, I realize that endless aspects of existence are waiting to be discovered and that life is art in progress, a textbook with wisdom on every page. The knowledge to be found is never ending, and with each day I evolve. Seen from this vantage point, I cannot fail—I can only learn and grow.

*December 13, 2000:* The long shadows cast over the yard remind me that an entire season has passed since my return to my father's house. As surely as autumn has turned to winter, it seems we too progress to ever new seasons in our lives—a planting, the cultivation and harvest, the ensuing sleep in the soft darkness of the earth's bed. Those of us undefeated by the brutality of our past can then hoist ourselves up to greet the slanting rays of possibility that gain visibility across the horizon.

In early autumn when I first arrived, blustery winds would at times surge through the walls of my father's house, causing a bitter chill and blowing leaves, scorched and brittle, through every open portal. Yet now, even the blanketing snows bring a hint of warmth. I could leave as soon as tomorrow, but then I would miss the rising of the sap in the tree trunks and the chance to savor whatever sweetness there is to be gathered. During my childhood and adolescence, there was no sweetness. Distanced from my spiritual core and palpable sense of relationship with the outside world, I knew only the physicality of my being—with which I was obsessed. I was acutely aware, for example, that the 5.6 calories in a stick of gum had to be painstakingly earned and that starvation gave me a way to gain control over my body, something I was deprived of as a child. And while I did not yet know that the energy holding the cycle of addiction in place was concealing an ocean of pain, my greatest desire was to get out of this dungeon of a house.

Now, however, I think I will stay a while, no longer as a casualty of the past but as a promising candidate for a vital future. As a victim I had let unfortunate circumstances and people who had wronged me win my internal tug-of-war; as a survivor I am the victor. More specifically, by admitting defeat, I had allowed a curable disorder to overpower my will to live. Yet by learning to identify the origin of the problem and take control of my violent impulses, I have transformed from lost to found—from a teenager depending fully on her family to ensure her survival to a young adult finally able to reciprocate the love they showered on me all this time.

As a result, new family bonds are forming and I am at last able to articulate my appreciation to the people who sustained me throughout my ordeal. I am grateful for my mother's abiding support, my brother's extraordinary offerings of love, my sister's unwavering protection, and my father's unconditional generosity. At times this freshly woven web of relations strains at the tug of unshared perceptions and unfulfilled expectations, especially regarding rates and methods of recovery. Nevertheless, it steadfastly supports a fabric to which I can contribute, as an equal partner, from a self no longer marinating in distress.

I take no pride in my conduct over these twelve years of my life; nor do I harbor shame over it. In fact, for the first time ever I genuinely love myself. Having emerged from the clouds of secrecy and the caves of darkness, I can see that the more I face the sunshine in any situation, the more the shadows fall behind me.

# Anorexia Nervosa
## A Perspective for Parents

### Kathryn Weaver, PhD, RN

*P*arents struggle to cope with the intrusion of anorexia nervosa into their lives. A long, frightening illness, it challenges their comfort, values, sense of certainty—and worst of all, the life of their child. Feeling unqualified to help their son or daughter, many parents come to see themselves as powerless. Those who outgrow the resulting paralysis do so by mobilizing help for their child and eventually learning how to take charge.[1]

Taking charge entails attending simultaneously to the needs of the anorexic child and oneself—an endeavor requiring a parent to evolve from not knowing what to do to becoming a resource capable of helping everyone involved. Ultimately, parents who do this assist in clearing the way to their child's full recovery.

Mobilizing help for a child with anorexia nervosa evokes a wide range of emotional responses. At first, most parents become discouraged amidst the whirlwind of things to attend to—appointments with a variety of health professionals, batteries of diagnostic tests, decisions about who and when to tell, and juggling these tasks with other responsibilities. Parents worrying about their child's survival also tend to have many questions and few places to go for answers. In the face of their mounting responsibilities,

---

1. "Taking charge" is a term chosen by parents interviewed as part of the following study. K. Weaver, "Taking Charge: The Experience of Mothers Caring for Adolescent Daughters with Anorexia Nervosa" (University of New Brunswick, 2000).

it is easy to feel defeated by long waits, negative judgments, and lack of clear solutions.

In the early stages of seeking help for their child, most parents experience grief as well. They have lost the child they thought they knew. They have to some extent relinquished care of their child to professionals. They have lost their sense of security and may be too overwhelmed or saddened to talk to loved ones, preferring instead to access information and support online, where they can remain anonymous. Further losses are financial and temporal. Funds earmarked for other projects may have to be redirected to the child's health care even if the family has a health insurance policy. Vacation days may need to be diverted from time off to "time on" with the child. The future that many parents once envisioned is lost too, as their thoughts turn to the here-and-now exigencies of their child's eating disorder.

Often panic sets in. To strengthen their parenting bonds, most mothers and fathers quickly learn not to talk about eating or food in their child's presence, but they can be stymied about what *to* talk about. Having received conflicting advice from professionals, they can become further perplexed and frightened, wondering, "If starvation is the problem, why not try to feed her, much as I did when she was an infant?" Some parents, unable to resist resorting to enticement schemes, end up alienating their child.

To quell their sometimes terrifying uncertainty about doing the right thing, as well as their guilt over having possibly contributed to their child's crisis, fear regarding long-term health consequences, and remorse over having shortchanged their other children, many parents find ways to override their emotions. In response, they begin functioning less as caring parents and more as informal case managers operating in liaison with healthcare authorities and school officials. Parents describe this form of compensation as "switching to autopilot," or performing actions without mindfully attending to them.

Other parents acknowledge the emotional burden of caring for an anorexic child and try to adapt. One mother, who refers to this challenge as "doing the yo-yo act," explains: "When a good and bad thing are going on at the same time, you don't have the chance to be happy with the good situation, since you are simultaneously immersed in the difficult situation. For example, when I had one daughter graduating from high school and another hospitalized with anorexia, I felt torn between being elated and upset. My emotions went up and down like a yo-yo."

Still other parents actively suppress their emotions, especially any anger or frustration they may feel about being coerced into turning over household food management to their child with anorexia. Planning meal preparation and outings around a child's eating behaviors can become infuriating. An exasperated father might note: "When I'm cooking dinner, my son is constantly in my face, saying things like 'Why don't you add this ingredient,' or 'Why don't you make it that way.' And then he doesn't eat it anyway, so what's the point?" Attempting to balance a child's unrealistic demands with larger family considerations can be annoying under any circumstances, but when the child has a food disorder and the demands are made in the kitchen, it can be maddening, driving many sensitive parents to emotional containment.

Whether a parent resorts to autopilot, the yo-yo effect, or containment, struggling to meet the ongoing care demands of a child with anorexia is likely to culminate in mental exhaustion, or burnout. Symptoms center around feeling ineffective against the magnitude of tasks required without seeing positive results or receiving recognition for efforts made. Preparing a child's favorite foods while unobtrusively attempting to monitor the child's nutritional and emotional status—a juggling act that does not resolve the eating disorder—can easily increase a parent's anxiety. The underlying cause for the eventual burnout is usually that the parent has been striving to meet everyone's emotional needs but his or her own.

In transitioning from mobilizing help for the child to taking charge, parents learn to direct energy to their own needs by setting limits on caregiving and by engaging with other parents who face similar challenges. Setting limits means reducing the degree of involvement in activities such as mediating between family members, curtailing the torrent of non-helpful advice from others, and releasing any guilt associated with taking time for oneself. Sharing experiences and feelings with parents of other children with anorexia can be equally rewarding, either individually or in community groups. Giving voice to the parenting experience aids not only others setting forth on the challenge but oneself as well, since it feels good to serve as a resource.

Taking charge, however, does not come naturally. It is essential to plan for it and work consistently at it.

### How to Take Charge When Your Child Has Been Diagnosed with Anorexia Nervosa

✳ List your questions and concerns about your child's food behaviors. Then discuss each item on your list privately with the professionals caring for your child.

✳ Establish mealtime rules: Will your child cook? Will only your child's "safe foods" be served? Will separate meals be prepared? Once you've stated the rules, stick to them.

✳ Read everything you can about anorexia nervosa. Ask therapists to recommend books. Visit the Web sites of national organizations for additional information.

✳ Understand that many factors contribute to the development of an eating disorder and that you may never be able to successfully identify the precise cause for your child's difficulties with food.

✳ Collaborate whenever possible with the professionals who are caring for your child. Participate in therapies when invited; ask to be included in team meetings; work with the primary therapist to help educate your child's teachers, coaches, and school authorities.

✳ Regard each experience at home as an opportunity to enhance your family's well-being by stimulating long-term change and growth.

✳ Interact frequently with your child rather than the eating disorder. Express interest in your child as a person and discuss things that he or she considers important.

✳ Generate a personal support system of individuals you feel comfortable talking to, such as professional caregivers, friends, family members, or a combination of all three.

✳ Learn to discharge anger and other troublesome emotions through physical activity, like sports, walking, gardening, construction, or arts and crafts. Engage in activities that provide fulfillment and boost self-esteem: pursue a hobby, read a good book, go on family outings, raise a pet. Avoid situations that do not nourish you with compassion and support, such as talking to people who pump you for information about your child.

✳ Record your parenting experiences in a journal. Over time, look for changes in the big picture rather than its isolated components. This can help you regard one stressful event or bad day as just that rather than losing sight of the overall pattern of successes.

✳ Learn where your control ends and your child's autonomy begins. Rather than policing your child's food intake, bathroom time, and physical activity, encourage her to plan and implement her own recovery strategies. Allow for plenty of trial and error as she determines what works for her particular situation.

✳ Do not expect recovery to occur within a fixed time span. Recovery unfolds over a period of years and varies from one child to the next.

✳ Keep a record of the helpful responses people have given you. Share these freely, along with additional forms of encouraging feedback, as you become an expert helping others on the journey.

*Kathryn Weaver, PhD, RN, is an assistant professor and nurse psychotherapist special-izing in anorexia nervosa and the provision of long-term therapy for eating disorders at the Faculty of Nursing, University of New Brunswick, Canada.*

# About the Author

Sara Jane Thornton is a writer, speaker, and child-care provider who lives in New Brunswick, Canada. An advocate for the rights of mental health patients and sexual abuse survivors, she focuses much of her work on revealing the underlying realities of eating disorders.

At age sixteen, following years of childhood sexual abuse, Sara dropped out of school, left home, and developed alcohol, drug, and sex addictions, eventually sliding into a downward spiral of self-starvation that nearly took her life. Hospitalized at twenty-one for a medley of psychiatric ailments including anorexia, bulimia, obsessive-compulsive disorder, depression, and borderline personality disorder, she was given a dismal prognosis. Aided by her innate resilience and determination, she defied expectations and, discharged at age twenty-three, began learning to live on her own.

She subsequently graduated with honors from New Brunswick Community College. She then worked as a crisis counselor for at-risk youth, at an agency where she met her future husband, Chris, a fellow counselor, and at age twenty-six she gave birth to a daughter named Fallon.

Sara currently plans to pursue a PhD in clinical psychology at the University of New Brunswick, where she has served as a guest speaker. Her triumphant struggle with anorexia has been featured in newspaper articles, and she is one of three women appearing in the film *Through True Eyes: Process of Recovery from Eating Disorders,* produced by Atlantic Mediaworks.

Please visit www.facingthesunshine.com for more information on Sara's work and appearances.

# Order Form

Appelstein Training Resources (ATR) provides strength-based materials to help better understand and respond to the needs of at-risk children and youth. The items listed below, other than *Facing the Sunshine*, were either written or produced by ATR's president, Charles Appelstein, MSW.

| Quantity | Amount |
|---|---|
| **Books** | |
| _____ *Facing the Sunshine: A Young Woman's Emergence from the Shadows of Sexual Abuse and Anorexia* ($19.95) | _____ |
| _____ *No Such Thing As a Bad Kid: Understanding and Responding to the Challenging Behavior of Troubled Children and Youth* ($19.95) | _____ |
| _____ *The Gus Chronicles: Reflections from an Abused Kid* ($12.00) | _____ |
| _____ *The Gus Chronicles II: Reflections from a Kid Who Has Been Abused* ($12.00) | _____ |
| **CDs** | |
| _____ *One-Line Raps for Girls and Chaps: Rhythmic Self-Talk to Help Children and Youth Self-Manage* ($12.95) | _____ |
| **Training Videos** | |
| _____ *Creating and Maintaining a Strength-Based Environment* ($69.95) | _____ |
| _____ *Managing Number One and Putting In the Bricks* ($149.95) | _____ |
| _____ *Key Concepts for Preventing Problem Behavior & Building Self-Esteem in Troubled Children and Youth* ($59.95) | _____ |
| _____ Complete set of training videotapes ($250.00) | _____ |
| Subtotal | _____ |

Balance forward      _____

Shipping and handling $2.50 _____
*(No charge for orders over $25.00)*

**Total amount of order**      _____

*Quantity discounts available*

---

### Method of payment:

☐ Check or money order enclosed (made payable to **Appelstein Training Resources** in US funds only)

☐ MasterCard               ☐ VISA

Credit Card #_____Exp._____

### Ship to (please print):

NAME_____

ADDRESS_____

CITY/STATE/ZIP_____

PHONE_____

# ATR

*Hope Is Humanity's Fuel*

Appelstein Training Resources, LLC
12 Martin Avenue • Salem, NH 03079
Phone/fax: 603-898-5573
www.charliea.com